2 50

6c

PRAISE FOR *YOUR BLUEPRINT FOR LIFE*

"Your Blueprint for Life is a brilliant book for anyone seeking to discover God's full potential for his or her life. Michae. Kendrick provides strategic steps that lead us into a closer relationship w th God."

—LOUIE GIGLIO, SENIOR PASTOR, PASSION CITY CHURCH, ATLANTA, GEORGIA, AND FOUNDER, PASSION CONFERENCES

"In Your Blueprint for Life, Mike Kendrick has challenged us to live with intention and focus on those things that matter: our relationship with God and our relationships with others. This book provides a practical guide to centering your life around those things that will matter in eternity. I have seen Mike live this out. I have had the privilege of being on the King's Ridge Christian School Board, and he motivated and challenged all of us in this process. Mike has truly impacted my life, and through this book, he will yours as well."

—JOHN SMOLTZ, FORMER Cy YOUNG AWARD–WINNING MAJOR LEAGUE BASEBALL PITCHER AND MEMBER OF THE NATIONAL BASEBALL HALL OF FAME

"If you have struggled to understand your purpose and calling in life, *Your Blueprint for Life* is for you. Mike Kendrick has developed a practical and effective guide to help you understand how God has uniquely created you for His purposes. Read *Your Blueprint for Life*, and it will help you align your priorities around those things that will matter in eternity."

—ANDY STANLEY, SENIOR PASTOR, NORTH POINT COMMUNITY CHURCH, ALPHARETTA, GEORGIA

"Your Blueprint for Life focuses on the importance of living a life that will outlast you, a life with purpose. Life is short, but God has placed each of us here to make a difference. To impact lives for eternity, we all need a blueprint to follow. Without a plan we will aimlessly wander around without reaching our potential. *Your Blueprint for Life* gives clear examples and truths to use on your life's journey. This book is a must read for anyone who wants to align their passions, gifts, and calling with eternity in mind."

—DR. JOHNNY HUNT, SENIOR PASTOR, FIRST BAPTIST CHURCH, WOODSTOCK, GEORGIA

"The magnificent thing about God's principles as revealed in His Word is that they are timeless and transcendent. They always work, will never change, and are always relevant. Mike Kendrick has written a book that shows how biblical principles can be worked out in a practical, challenging, and thoroughly biblical way in all of the significant areas of life. I would encourage anyone to make this book one to read every year. It will change your life."

—RON BLUE, AUTHOR, SPEAKER, AND FOUNDER OF RON BLUE INSTITUTE, KINGDOM ADVISORS, AND RON BLUE & CO.

Your
BLUEPRINT
for
LIFE

Your

BLUEPRINT

for

LIFE

HOW TO ALIGN YOUR PASSION, GIFTS, AND CALLING WITH ETERNITY IN MIND

MICHAEL KENDRICK

NELSON
BOOKS

An Imprint of Thomas Nelson

Published in Nashville, Tennessee, by Nelson Books, an imprint of Thomas Nelson. Nelson Books and Thomas Nelson are registered trademarks of HarperCollins Christian Publishing, Inc.

Author is represented by the literary agency of Yates & Yates, 1100 Town & Country Road, Suite 1300, Orange, California 92868.

Interior designed by James A. Phinney.

Thomas Nelson Inc. titles may be purchased in bulk for educational, business, fund-raising, or sales promotional use. For information, please e-mail SpecialMarkets@ThomasNelson.com.

Unless otherwise noted, Scripture quotations are taken from the NEW KING JAMES VERSION. © 1982 by Thomas Nelson, Inc. Used by permission. All rights reserved.

Scripture quotations marked NIV are taken from the Holy Bible, New International Version®, NIV®. Copyright © 1973, 1978, 1984, 2011 by Biblica, Inc.™ Used by permission of Zondervan. All rights reserved worldwide. www.zondervan.com

Scripture quotations marked NASB are taken from the NEW AMERICAN STANDARD BIBLE®. © The Lockman Foundation 1960, 1962, 1963, 1968, 1971, 1972, 1973, 1975, 1977, 1995. Used by permission.

Scripture quotations marked TLB are taken from *The Living Bible.* © 1971. Used by permission of Tyndale House Publishers, Inc., Wheaton, Illinois 60189. All rights reserved.

Scripture quotations marked NLT are taken from the *Holy Bible*, New Living Translation. © 1996. Used by permission of Tyndale House Publishers, Inc., Wheaton, Illinois 60189. All rights reserved.

Library of Congress Cataloging-in-Publication Data

Kendrick, Michael, 1960-
  Your blueprint for life : how to align your passion, gifts, and calling with eternity in mind / Michael Kendrick.
    pages cm
  ISBN 978-1-4002-0660-5
1. Christian life. I. Title.
  BV4501.3.K4584 2015
  248.4--dc23

2014038440

Printed in the United States of America

15 16 17 18 19 RRD 6 5 4 3 2 1

CONTENTS

CONTENTS

Chapter One

YOUR BLUEPRINT
FOR LIFE

HAVE YOU NOTICED THAT EVERYONE longs to be more than they are? The desire to succeed, to make one's mark on the world, and to live a life that counts is like a burning flame God placed in the human heart.

Maybe this desire to be more and do something meaningful with our lives is why we love movies like *The Lord of the Rings*, *Apollo 13*, and *Braveheart*, as well as the Bible stories of Paul, Joseph, and Esther. These messages speak to something deep inside us that tells us we were created to make a difference, not just float through life then die without making a mark.

I'll bet you want to do something significant with your life too. You want to leave a legacy and make a difference for God. You want your life to count.

Ever since I was small, I have experienced this burning just described. At times it has burned red hot; other times it has been less obvious—but I have always felt it, and it has shown up in my desire to be anything but normal.

For me, "normal" has always been defined as a status-quo, boring, insignificant, and unfulfilled life—and that's definitely not what I wanted.

Maybe I wanted to avoid the status quo of ordinary at all costs because I grew up on a farm outside the normal, small southern town of Enterprise, Alabama. Maybe it was because my parents worked nine to five for the government throughout their careers. By the time I reached high school, my determination to make a mark on the world grew when I wasn't even a mention in my high school yearbook.

After high school graduation, I decided I would try to avoid a status-quo life and that I would make my mark on the world by enrolling in the aerospace engineering program at Auburn University. I chose aerospace engineering because I'd always enjoyed math, and I figured rockets were the fastest way to get wherever I was going.

With my degree in hand, I quickly landed a job with Pratt & Whitney aircraft in West Palm Beach, Florida. Imagine the response when I told people my new job was developing the most advanced military aircraft in the world.

My fear of being ordinary made itself obvious on my first day on the job. I wouldn't say the division where I reported was a cubicle farm, but something about it reeked of predictability. In my mind, it represented the kind of normalcy I had vowed to escape.

As I looked across the office, I could practically mark out the years in cubicles. My cube represented year one—entry level. Eleven feet away, my boss's cube represented the twenty-year mark. And seventeen feet beyond that, my boss's boss sat at the thirty-year mark.

The rest of my life was to be a twenty-eight-foot journey from a small cubicle to a medium one to a large one. No matter how hard I worked or how much I accomplished, I would never go any farther in life than twenty-eight feet. It felt almost morbid. And it was more than I could bear.

This fear of normalcy burning deep in my soul led me to quit my job (much to my parents' chagrin) and eventually led me on an exciting career path in business. And then one day—because God had blessed me financially—I was able to stop working thirty years before my expected retirement date. I was thrilled! I could sleep in whenever I wanted, golf anytime, and occasionally sit by the swimming pool. What could be better? There didn't seem to be anything normal about that!

I also thought God had financially prospered me so I could serve Him in full-time ministry. So I spent a substantial amount of time every week volunteering for worthy causes. I served at a large church in Atlanta as a cameraman. I volunteered at a nationwide pro-life organization with a mission to save unborn children, and I feverishly helped a national political organization to elect Christian candidates to office.

I thought these ways of serving God would give me the satisfaction I was seeking and would satisfy the burning. I assumed that having more free time, managing my own schedule, and being financially independent would cause my happiness quotient to soar off the charts.

But it didn't. I was completely miserable.

After twelve long months of dreading each day, I decided to go back into business. I obtained my license as a registered investment advisor and became an investment banker. Thankfully, my anxiety disappeared and was replaced with passion. I was so thrilled about doing business again that I didn't even mind waking up at three or four in the morning so I could talk with overseas European investors. That decision to reengage in business turned out to be one of the best decisions I ever made.

Don't get me wrong. I love Christ, and He is the reason for everything I do, which is why I wondered why I was so miserable in ministry but felt fulfilled and alive in business.

When I discovered why, I finally understood how to experience true satisfaction and fulfillment and satisfy the burning in my heart. I finally understood why God created me! I also learned how to align my passions, gifts, and calling with eternity in mind.

When I learned through Scripture that God will reward us in heaven for how we steward our lives on the earth, my joy skyrocketed. My life took on even more meaning because I began to make the connection between using my gifts and talents for Christ and making an impact on heaven. This new understanding led me to launch multiple organizations, including Blueprint for Life, which is dedicated to helping others live with purpose in light of eternity—and it's why I am writing this book.

Maybe you feel unfulfilled as I did and have a burning desire to be more than you are. Let me encourage you. You *can* experience fulfillment. You *can* live with purpose. And you can answer the questions, "Why am I here?" and "Why do I exist?" You can satisfy your burning to make a mark and live for Christ. You just need a blueprint for your life.

What's in a Blueprint?

Maybe you have heard the term *blueprint* in reference to a photographic print, usually on white paper, that shows the details of an architectural plan. Recently, these traditional blueprints have been replaced by more modern, less-expensive digital images. Regardless of how they are created, a blueprint shows the builder how to build the house.

When my wife and I built our home, our architect presented us with a set of blueprints that showed how our new house would be designed. It showed the bedrooms, how high the walls would be, and where my man cave for watching football games would be located.

In the upcoming pages, I will help you create a blueprint too. Not for your new house, but for your entire life. This powerful life plan will show you what God the Architect had in mind when He designed you. It will also show you how to align your passions, gifts, and calling with eternity in mind *and* support all three through five important life areas: spiritual, relational, physical, financial, and career—what I call the Big Five. Not only that, but you'll discover how you can experience fulfillment now, not just after you meet Christ face-to-face.

By developing your personal Blueprint for Life, you will also be able to:

- Identify your gifts and passions to fulfill your *calling*
- Develop a *spiritual plan* for maximum intimacy with Christ
- Leverage and manage your *finances and earthly assets* to make a difference now and for eternity
- Choose and develop a *career path* to support—rather than take away from—your calling
- Develop an intentional plan to nurture and support your most important *relationships*
- Maximize your *physical health* to give you the stamina you need to fulfill your calling

Here are a few other main points about your Blueprint for Life.

It will help you live intentionally.

Imagine that it's a sunny Saturday afternoon in June. You have a few free hours so you decide to go rafting a couple of miles from your home. You call your best buddy and invite him to join you. Within the hour he knocks on your front door. You take him to the garage and he helps you pack what you need for your excursion:

the raft, two life jackets, bottled water, sunscreen, a couple of towels, and your sack lunches. After everything is loaded in your truck, your friend looks around and asks, "Where are the paddles?"

"Oh, we're not taking any," you respond. "We don't need them. We are just going to let the river take us wherever."

Your friend raises an eyebrow, stares at you, and gives you an "Are-you-crazy?" look. Everyone knows that no one goes rafting without paddles. You need them for guidance. Without them, you'll end up stuck in some trees along the river, or sucked into a current, and you'll definitely miss your destination.

It's tragic that a lot of people float the river of life without any "paddles." They don't have a plan. The river of life takes them wherever it wills; they live without intention. As a result, they often feel like their existence is pointless. If you feel as though you are floating down the river of life without intention, your Blueprint for Life will help you change that so you can live with purpose.

I already mentioned that many people live unsatisfied lives. But have you ever truly considered why? Other than not living out their calling, like I wasn't when I was sitting by the pool, there is something deeper than that.

It's the hole in your soul—and everyone alive has one.

This is the longing that may sometimes make you feel as though you are incomplete and that God made a mistake when He knit you together in your mother's womb, but He didn't. Instead, He strategically placed this void inside you as a gift. This is what I call the "hole in your soul."

Perhaps if God chose to speak to you about this, He would say:

I know there are times you feel frustrated with your life. I subjected My creation to frustration in hope that it would find Me

(Rom. 8:19–21). If you were self-sufficient, if you didn't have an ache, a longing for something more, why would you ever seek Me? This hole in your soul is My gift to you. It's My way of drawing you to Myself and inviting you to participate in My plans. After sin entered the garden, I was so deeply grieved that I had to find a way to draw you back to Myself, to make you want Me and My will, so I subjected mankind to frustration, to a feeling of being incomplete. I know it can hurt, but when you allow it to push you to seek Me, and you seek Me with all your heart, then you will find Me (Jer. 29:13)—and you will experience joy.

Some people allow the hole in their soul to push them to false loves, idols of the heart, like sex, drugs, or prestige. But it's only when they allow their dissatisfaction to push them to Me that they can find the highest level of satisfaction possible in this life. Will you allow the hole in your soul to drive you into My arms and into My plan for you?

You can live a purposeful, joy-filled existence, not *in spite of* the hole in your soul, but *because of* it. And developing your Blueprint for Life will help fill that hole.

It will help you leverage your passions, gifts, and calling with eternity in mind.

One day your body or "earth suit" will give out and you will slip out of it like a pair of pajamas. The breath of God in you will return to God and you will meet your Maker. Paul said, "So we are always confident, knowing that while we are at home in the body we are absent from the Lord" (2 Cor. 5:6).

You will meet the One who created the majestic Rocky Mountains, babies, dogs, and butterflies—and you. And in that moment, the opportunities you had to make a difference for Christ and use your passions, gifts, and calling for Him will be gone, never to be recovered. Your moments will be swallowed up in time.

That may not seem like a big deal because the earth and all its troubles will be a distant memory. After all, if you are a Christian, you will slide into eternity in bliss and nothing that you did on earth will matter in heaven anyway, right? Wrong. If you are in Christ, true, your sins have been forgiven and your punishment has been paid for, but everything good you did on the earth will matter in a big way in heaven. This is why it matters how you steward your life.

In his book *A Life God Rewards*, Bruce Wilkinson wrote,

> Have you ever sat, eyes glued to the television watching the Olympic awards ceremony with tears streaming down your cheeks? I have. There is something about the scene that pulls at a person's heart.
>
> Your favorite athlete climbs the steps of the awards platform, her national anthem fills the stadium, her nation's flag waves in the spotlight. Her years of sweat and self-denial have paid off. She has finished her race. And she has won. Now, as thousands applaud, an Olympic official drapes a medal around her neck.
>
> One day you and I will have our own rewards ceremony in eternity. The halls of heaven will ring with praise and celebration. Witnesses from every nation and every generation will watch with eager anticipation. Even angels will pause.[1]

When your time on earth is over, if you are a Christ follower, it will be your turn to stand on the platform to receive your rewards for what you have done on the earth—including how you have used your passions, gifts, and calling for God. Second Corinthians 5:10 says, "For we must all appear before the judgment seat of Christ, that each one may receive the things done in the body, according to what he has done, whether good or bad." When I wake each morning and walk to the bathroom to brush my teeth, I see a little motivational quote next to the sink that reminds me that I don't have long to make an impact for Jesus. It says, "Every Second Counts." I try to remember to ask myself the question: *What will I do today that will matter in eternity?*

Because everything you do on the earth will matter in heaven, it's important to live intentionally with eternity in mind. Your Blueprint for Life will help you do that very thing.

It will help align your life with God's plans.

Have you noticed that moms tell their kids the things that are important? "Johnny, make sure you brush your teeth!" "Megan, don't run across the street!" "Samuel, be nice to that boy." Just like a good parent, God doesn't tell His kids what's important to Him without good reason. He tells them so they can participate in His plans. He wants them to do His will. He tells us love is His priority so we will be loving. He tells us money management is important so we will become good money managers. He tells us it's important to put Him first so we love Him above all else.

In the upcoming pages, you'll discover what's important to God so that you can participate in His plans by leveraging your passions, gifts, and calling for Him. Then you won't be floating down the river of life without making a difference in ways that truly matter. Instead, you can be a true success.

The good news is that God has equipped you to participate in what He cares about. When you know what God cares about, *and* you can identify your passions, gifts, and calling through your Blueprint for Life, you will have a better idea of how God wants to use you in His plans for the world.

THREE BIG RISKS

I am so convicted about helping you live a fulfilled life and make an impact for Christ that it's necessary to share a few things that are at risk if you *don't* pursue your Blueprint for Life.

You will sacrifice joy for happiness.

Maybe it doesn't sound bad to trade joy for happiness, but happiness isn't consistent; it comes and goes. You can experience it only when things are going well—and even then, it doesn't stick around. As soon as the initial excitement wears off, you'll need another shot of something good to bring happiness back. It's not fulfilling in the long run.

Thankfully, the joy that comes from developing your Blueprint for Life and pursuing your calling doesn't work that way. The joy God gives isn't dampened by gloomy weather or a bad economy, and it doesn't fade after the novelty is gone. It transcends life's circumstances. Joy is rooted in a deep sense of knowing who you belong to and that you are walking in His will. When you participate in His plans for your passions, gifts, and calling, you will find there is no greater joy because you will be partnering with the Creator of the universe. What could be more meaningful or bring more joy?

You will sacrifice full relationship with God for doing things your own way.

Again, maybe that doesn't sound like a bad trade, but knowing God and doing His will are inseparable concepts. If you claim to know God but don't engage in what He has prepared you to do, then you'll never have a fully developed relationship with Him. This doesn't mean you aren't a Christian. You can have a relationship with Christ even if you don't fulfill your calling. You just can't experience your relationship with Him in the fullness He intended.

Imagine a husband and wife who are committed to and love each other. Clearly, they can experience a genuine marriage relationship. But if they aren't on the same page in achieving their life's purposes, neither one of them is going to be fulfilled. There will always be a sense that something is missing.

Relationship with God is like that. We can talk to Him, hear from Him, and enjoy the relationship up to a point, but if we aren't on the same page with His calling for our lives, something will always be missing. We won't experience the partnership He designed for us. Like a premier athlete who sits on the sidelines or an eagle confined to a cage, we'll never use our gifts the way Christ intended. We'll never reach our full potential.

You will trade eternal rewards for temporary amusement.

The word *amusement* comes from the Latin word *muse*, which means "to think," and the prefix *a-*, which means "not." When our goal is temporary amusement, we're just not thinking. Admittedly, sometimes it can feel good not to think, to get away from the stresses of life. But it's like using a credit card. It will cost you more later if you make a habit of floating through life. That's a high price to pay.

Your salvation depends on placing your faith in Christ as your Lord and Savior, but as I mentioned, the Bible also says you will be rewarded in heaven based on how you accomplish His will (see 1 Cor. 3:11–15). What you do with your passions, gifts, and calling now will have a big impact in heaven later.

If you believed that your actions today would radically affect your experience in eternity, wouldn't it dramatically change how you think about life?

I hope you are looking forward to the journey ahead. In the upcoming chapters, I will help you align your passions, gifts, and calling—and support your calling with the Big Five areas of your life: spiritual, relational, physical, finances, and career. It's going to be a great ride as we create your Blueprint for Life together.

Let's get started! In the next chapter we'll talk about the real reason you are here and why you have been created.

Eternal Perspective Scripture

"If you say, 'Surely we did not know this,' does not He who weighs the hearts consider it? He who keeps your soul, does He not know it? And will He not render to each man according to his deeds?'" (Prov. 24:12).

Chapter Two

WHY AM I HERE?

S OME PEOPLE ARE DIRECTIONALLY CHALLENGED. They get lost going from one side of town to the other, from one side of the street to the other, or from one side of the grocery store to the other. It's easy for people who have more sophisticated internal compasses to make fun of these wandering folks, but the truth is that we are *all* directionally challenged if we don't know why we are here. If we have no answers to the questions "Why am I here?" and "Why have I been created?" we will all wander aimlessly through life.

The awesome news is that, contrary to what some people think, you *can* know why you are here. You *can* understand why you have been created. And once you know both of these things, you *can* live with purpose. You can align your passions, gifts, and calling. You don't have to be lost! Not only that, but once you understand why you are here, your calling—and how you manage the Big Five to support your calling—will also make sense.

In this chapter, I will reveal the two main reasons you have been created and why you have been placed on planet Earth. This is the first step in creating your Blueprint for Life. But to discover these truths, you need to come with me on a trip through the stars.

TO BETELGEUSE AND BEYOND

Imagine that you have been chosen to take a special trip with NASA to unexplored stars and galaxies. After you endure astronaut training, you suit up, then blast off traveling faster than the speed of light toward the star Alpha Centauri. This star is four and a half light-years away, or about 250,000 times the distance to the sun.

After stopping by Alpha Centauri, you zip through the Andromeda galaxy, which is more than 1.5 million light-years away. On the way there, you surf the Internet and learn that distant galaxies, which are visible through telescopes, are 6,500 million light-years away! You also learn that the sun is so large that one million spheres of the earth could fit inside it if it were hollow—but it's not the biggest star. You discover that some stars are so large that 500 million spheres of the sun could fit inside each one if they were hollow!

But your favorite star is Betelgeuse (pronounced "beetle juice")—and you can't wait to see it. It is 520 light-years from the earth, and it's one of the brightest stars of Orion's Belt. Its diameter is 500 million kilometers, which means that if it were hollow, the earth could comfortably revolve around the sun, *inside Betelgeuse*, in its normal orbit! After stopping by Betelgeuse, you step back into your rocket completely amazed, and then zip toward home through the Milky Way.

On the way back to earth, you marvel at the 100 million stars in your home galaxy—and that the sun is just one of them. When you think about the wonder of creation, that there are at least 100 million galaxies in the space that telescopes can see—and many more beyond—you feel very small, and God seems very big.

If God wanted to remain silent about His existence, He wouldn't have bothered creating the stars; He wouldn't have made the Milky Way, or Betelgeuse. In fact, He wouldn't have made the majestic Rocky Mountains, the rippling oceans, or the magnificent hummingbird. If His goal was to remain quiet and anonymous, He wouldn't have created anything at all.

Instead, He spoke a smorgasbord for our senses into existence. Wonder for our eyes, beauty for our ears, fragrances for our noses—and rapture for our hearts. His creation screams about His unseen beauty; it shouts about His unseen qualities and His magnificence.

When Michelangelo painted the ceiling of the Sistine Chapel, he crafted an outward expression of his inner person. In the same way, God's creation exhibited through the mountains, stars, and oceans is an expression of the God we can't see.

The Bible says, "The heavens declare the glory of God; and the firmament shows His handiwork" (Ps. 19:1). Anything less grand would not have been a true representation of Himself—His indescribable, unfathomable, indefinable glory.

God didn't remain anonymous because He didn't want to. Rather, He wanted to display His glory throughout the universe as His gift to man. Once you understand this, you'll be able to understand the two main reasons you are here.

TO GLORIFY GOD

It seems that it would have been enough for God to glorify Himself through the stars, but He didn't stop there. Instead, after He created the heavens and the earth, the Bible says He created something even more amazing.

He scooped some dirt from the ground He had made and formed the very first man. It was a sacred moment. Adam was a first edition. Nothing like this had been done before. God bent over the lifeless Adam and breathed into him to give man His spirit. He imparted Himself to man, as a mother is a part of a child.

A holy hush must have traveled through heaven. This was

God's crown of creation. The breath of God in man, wrapped in human flesh.

In the same way that God created the universe to display His glory, God created people to display His glory too. In Psalm 139:14 the psalmist says that he is "fearfully and wonderfully made." To be fearfully and wonderfully made means that you are beyond figuring out. You are a divine mystery of God. You are God's fingerprint and an expression of His glory. Wow!

Consider these facts about how you have been created. In the *Bread of Life Study*, it says:

> Doctors tell us that the human brain has 30 billion nerve-cells, each operating at a potential of nearly one-tenth of a volt of electricity. Those over 35 years of age lose 1,000 of these nerve cells every day—and these cells are never replaced. Yet the main functions of the brain carry on till the end of life, even though there is a slight loss in the sensitivity of the five senses.
>
> Did you know that each of our eyes has 130 million little rods for black and white vision and 7 million cones for color vision? These are connected to the brain by 300,000 nerve fibers. The human eye can receive 1.5 million messages simultaneously! To duplicate the function of one eye mechanically, it would require 250,000 television transmitters and receivers!
>
> Now look at the heart and the blood vessels. We don't usually think of them until they give us some trouble! But that heart which God has put within our bodies beats 40 million times every year, without any lubrication and without taking a vacation. Even though you didn't realize it, your heart beat within your body 100,000 times yesterday, pumping blood through 100,000 kilometers of blood vessels from your head to your feet. Your body

also produced more than 172 billion red blood cells just yesterday to replace the damaged and worn-out cells. Isn't it a miracle that you are alive today?

In every cell of your body, there is a very detailed instruction code. There are three billion letters of DNA code determining your hair color, how you laugh, the color of your eyes, and if you are short or tall in every cell of your body. Therefore, DNA is a three-billion-lettered program telling the cell to act in a certain way. It is a full instruction manual.[1]

It's clear that when God created the universe and then man that His intent was to display His glory. His creation is so amazing that it cries out, "To God be the glory!"

This is the first reason you are here and why you have been created: you are here to glorify God.

To glorify Him means that you put the spotlight on Him and you leverage everything you can in your life to lift Him up so others can see Him. You maximize all that you have been given to show and tell others about Him. You use your passions, your gifts, your calling, and all that you are and have. If you make this your goal, you will experience a deep joy and fulfillment that cannot in any way come from selfishly serving yourself.

Some people think that saying God wants to be glorified makes Him sound like an egomaniac, but they are missing the point because God's love is not opposed to God's glory; God's glory *is* God's gift to man. It's His love spilling all over us through His creation. This gift of God's glory is how He often woos us and draws us to Himself the way a lover woos his beloved. So you see, God is not an egomaniac; He is a *giver*.

Maybe you're thinking, *Well, Mike. I have heard God wants me to glorify Him, but I don't have any idea how to do that.* We'll talk about how you can specifically glorify Him through your passions, gifts, and calling in the upcoming chapters.

HE CAME

History is filled with great love stories. But the greatest love story of all time trumps all others. It's the story of the God who created the Milky Way and Betelgeuse coming to the earth to die for those He created even though they had rejected Him. It's a passionate love story of God pursuing people.

Have you ever wondered why He went to so much trouble, why He bothered with the horror of the cross? After all, since He is God and is obviously in charge, He could have taken an easier road. He could have demanded love from His creation. He could have made love mandatory. But He didn't. Instead, He did the unthinkable.

He willingly died.

In blood and brutality.

At the hands of people who falsely accused Him.

He was beaten.

Beyond recognition.

Mocked.

And nailed to a tree.

Between two criminals.

God proved His love through action. Anything less would have been an incorrect representation of His love and not a true expression of His heart. Anyone who goes to so much trouble to prove love has one motive: to win love. True love is always proven by action.

This is the main reason Christ came: to have a love relationship with those He created—including you. So, this is the second reason you are here: to know Christ and have an intimate love relationship with Him.

TO KNOW CHRIST

Joe and Judy live in the same house. They are married and share a bed. They move silently past each other every morning in the hall and brush their teeth over the same sink—but they never exchange any communication. They are strangers sharing square footage.

So it is with some people who attend church. Every Sunday they come into God's house. They hear *about* Him, but they never *hear* Him. They speak *of* Him, but they never speak *with* Him. Their "relationship" with God isn't genuine, which grieves the One who died to prove His love.

God doesn't want you to know *about* Him; He wants you to intimately *know* Him. And, only when you truly know Him can you truly glorify Him. The two main reasons you are here go hand in hand.

To have a genuine relationship with Christ means you communicate with Him. You tell others about Him because you are proud of Him. You think about how you can please Him, and you demonstrate your love, just as a man who loves his wife demonstrates his. God wants you to discover what's important to Him by reading the Bible, which is His love letter to you. He wants you to talk with Him and allow Him to speak to you through Scripture and the Holy Spirit. He wants you to share your ongoing life story with Him. This is the context in which intimacy grows.

Intimacy isn't just for earthly relationships; it's also for relationship with God. Some people believe that because they can't see God they can't have a real relationship with Him. You may not be able to see Him, but you can have an intimate, vibrant relationship with Him that is as real to you as one with your best friend.

In the early morning hours, I spend time reading my Bible and I turn my attention toward God. I pray for Him to speak to me through His Word—and during this time I am often reminded why I have been created.

I have been created to be a businessman, husband, father, and friend. But more than anything, I have been created to be God's child. There are times when I sit with Him that a deep satisfaction swells over me. *Yes, this is what I was created for. This is why I am here. This is where I belong.* There is nothing this side of heaven like knowing the One who knows me through and through.

I can find a lot of happiness in this world, but there is nothing that rivals the intimacy I have with my Creator. Without a relationship with Christ, nothing else in life would make sense. My career in business would be a complete waste of time without knowing Him; He is the foundation for all I do.

In Philippians 3:8 Paul wrote, "I consider everything a loss compared to the surpassing greatness of knowing Christ Jesus my Lord, for whose sake I have lost all things" (NIV). God wants this to be true of you and me as well. To understand this is to begin to understand how to experience a sense of purpose and the greatest fulfillment and joy possible this side of heaven.

I want to add something very important: because God desires a relationship with you, He doesn't want the leftovers of your life. He doesn't want your leftover affections and loyalties after you give your time and energy to friends, finances, work, your children, your mate, school, the government, television, Twitter, or Facebook.

Relationship and commitment to Christ cannot be Jesus and money, Jesus and sex, Jesus and my BMW, Jesus and my career. He wants to be your top priority.

In America, we've gotten used to mixing relationship with Christ with other affections that rival Him, and we think it's okay. The result has been a watered-down version of what Jesus intended when He said, "Come, follow Me."

GETTING IT STRAIGHT

Glorifying Christ and knowing Christ are the foundation of your Blueprint for Life. Without either as a priority, you will not experience the joy Christ desires and nothing in your life will make sense. But let me clarify something: though I listed knowing Christ as our second reason for being here, with glorifying God as the first, knowing Christ must come first in your life because you can't truly glorify Him unless you first know Him.

Jesus said, "Apart from me you can do nothing" (John 15:5 NIV). This means you can't do anything that will produce any lasting fruit in His kingdom without knowing Him. Anything else will just produce dead fruit.

It's a common mistake for even Christians to seek their calling apart from their relationship with God. They may have accepted Christ, but their real passion is for what they *do*, not for the One who created them. Remember, there is no way you can fully live out your calling apart from Christ, because it's His calling for your life that you seek.

In his book *The Purpose Driven Life*, Rick Warren wrote,

The purpose of your life is far greater than your own personal fulfillment, your peace of mind, or even your happiness. It's far greater than your family, your career, or even your wildest dreams and ambitions. If you want to know why you were placed on this planet, you must begin with God. You were born *by* his purpose and *for* his purpose.[2]

THE HOLE IN YOUR SOUL

Do you remember that I talked about the "hole in your soul" in the first chapter? That's the longing that sometimes makes you feel incomplete and as if God made a mistake when He knit you together in your mother's womb. God strategically placed this hole inside you as a gift, because He wants to fill it when you have an intimate relationship with Him *and* you glorify Him. Developing your Blueprint for Life will help fill this hole.

Please don't misunderstand. I am not saying you can live a trouble-free existence. That won't happen until you go home to heaven. But I am saying you can experience great joy knowing you are aligned with your Architect and what He had in mind when He designed you.

I am also not saying any works you do to glorify God save you. Scripture clearly states, "by grace you have been saved, through faith—and this is not from yourselves, it is the gift of God" (Eph. 2:8 UPDATED NIV). But I am saying that true love is proven by action and that "faith without works is dead" (James 2:20). Without demonstrating your love to Him, you won't experience the full life God desires.

When I was fourteen years old, I landed my first big job as a paper boy for the *Daily Ledger* in Enterprise, Alabama. I still remember the elation and thrill I experienced when I received fifty dollars after working for one month. Getting up at 4:00 a.m. on Sunday morning to deliver papers, sometimes in the cold and rain, seemed a small price to pay for such a lucrative sum.

Little did I know at the time that such hard work would lay the groundwork to purchase, at age sixteen, my first car. It was a silver Pontiac Firebird with an orange stripe down the side. After the salesman handed me the keys and I drove it off the lot, the first thing I did was fill up the gas tank. Then I took it out for a long drive. It was summer, so I rolled down the windows, cranked up the stereo, and went on a driving adventure because that is what you do when you are sixteen and you get some new wheels.

Having a relationship with Jesus without fulfilling your calling is like filling up your car with gas and letting it sit in the driveway. You'll miss out on an adventure with God, expressing your love to Him through action, and the fulfillment that only partnering with Him to bring Him glory can bring.

In John 10:10, Jesus said, "I have come that they [that's you and me] may have life, and have it to the full" (NIV). God wants to bless you with a full, joy-filled life when you know Him and participate in His plans.

Here's a secret: You can sense God's love. You can go to church, raise your hands, and soak in hour after hour of Christian music. You can read your Bible and memorize scriptures and still feel unfulfilled, but God wants to give you full joy when you have an intimate relationship with Him *and* you glorify Him with your life by using your unique passions and gifts to do what He has called you to do.

The great news is that there is one way you can love Him and

27

glorify Him in a very special way like no one else can. This is the second step in building your Blueprint for Life the way the Architect intended.

"And whatever you do, do it heartily, as to the Lord and not to men, knowing that from the Lord you will receive the reward of the inheritance; for you serve the Lord Christ. But he who does wrong will be repaid for what he has done, and there is no partiality" (Col. 3:23–25).

Chapter Three

YOUR UNIQUE CALLING

MARCUS IS FRUSTRATED WITH LIFE. He wakes up at 6:00 a.m., drives to work, breathes in and out all day long, and lives for the weekend. He is a shipping agent for a large software company, and although he is pretty good at what he does, he still feels a nagging sense of dissatisfaction. He is well acquainted with the burning of wanting to be more. He doesn't want to just float through life. Like you and me, he wants his life to count.

One Sunday, he listened to a young woman at church share with the congregation that God had called her to be a nurse. For the last fifteen years of Marcus's professional life, he has heard stories like this and has prayed, "God, what have You called *me* to do?" He believes that knowing your calling must be for a chosen few and everyone else must be cursed with being frustrated for the rest of their lives. He has resigned himself to being miserable.

Maybe you can identify with Marcus. Maybe you doubt you have been created to do anything special for Him; and even if you do believe you have been called to serve Him, you have no idea how to discover your special passions and gifts.

In this chapter, I want to show you how to begin to identify your unique passions and gifts that will point you toward your calling. This is the one special way you can glorify Him like no one else can.

To begin, let's take a look at one of God's smallest creatures as a reminder that God has a calling for everyone—even you!

Even Bees Are Called

Every day outside the entrance of my office building, a flurry of bees hop from one colorful flower to another to forage for nectar. When a bee visits a flower some of the flower's pollen rubs off on the bee's belly. When the bee moves to the next flower, some of the pollen on his belly is transferred to that flower. Without this simple act of pollination can you imagine what would happen? Plants wouldn't give birth to seeds or fruit, crops would fail, and farmers would go bankrupt.

It's incredible that God Almighty, the Creator of heaven and earth, has given even the tiny bee a job to do! In fact, the bee's job is so important that approximately every three mouthfuls of food we enjoy is the direct result of pollination.

Doesn't it make logical sense that because God has a job for the tiny bee that He has a calling for you, the crown of His creation, too?

Your Unique Calling

There are a lot of ideas out there about what it means to have a calling. Believers in Christ have been called into God's kingdom, according to Ephesians 4:4, and we can be called to a vocation, according to 1 Corinthians 7:20. Some people think a calling can only be spiritual in nature such as serving in the pastorate, as a missionary, or as the leader for a Christian relief organization. Your calling can certainly be spiritual—rather than vocational or secular in nature. But God also calls people to be businessmen like me, stay-at-home moms, dentists, doctors, and dancers. We are all called to be important pieces of the puzzle He is creating in the world. When I talk about calling, I think this definition from Pastor Tony Evans works well: "[A calling is] the customized life purpose which God has ordained for you to bring Him the greatest glory and the maximum expansion of His kingdom."[1]

Ephesians 2:10 confirms that we all have a calling: "For we are God's workmanship, created in Christ Jesus to do good works, which God prepared in advance for us to do."

Prepared in Advance

Before God spoke the Milky Way into existence, before Betelgeuse, before the earth was placed on its axis, God planned you and He prepared you to do good works for Him.

There is something you can do that no one else can do quite like you, because God has uniquely equipped you for it.

Maybe you are thinking, *Well, lots of people do what I want to do.* True, there are many people who have the same calling. The world is filled with nurses and businessmen and engineers and flutists and dancers and pastors and writers and teachers. But remember that no one can do your calling quite like you because of the specific way God has created your personality, the physical abilities He has gifted you with, and even how He placed you in a particular geographic location. No one can reach the exact people you will reach every day for Him in the way you will reach them, at the exact time you will reach them. He uses people everywhere, and He wants to use you too for the plans He is carrying out in the world.

Now let's begin to define what your calling might be. Then, just as the tiny bee glorifies God through His special assignment, you can glorify Him too.

THE LIFE IMPACT TRIANGLE

Maybe like many people, understanding your calling has been the source of great anxiety and frustration. The good news is that there are clues to your calling written all over you because of the way God has created you. As Pastor Tony Evans has said, "Calling is tied to your creation."[2]

I am five feet nine inches tall. Imagine I want to be a center on a professional basketball team. As much as I want to play basketball, the way I have been designed is a good indication that I haven't been equipped to do so. I don't think the Celtics are looking for a shorty center. But there are other characteristics I possess that point me toward being a businessman. I love negotiating, developing new business ideas, and forming teams to start new businesses and ministries. These are clues to my calling.

You can begin to discover your unique calling by taking a look at the Life Impact Triangle. This triangle points you toward your God-given calling so you can make a big impact with your life for Christ, not just now, but for eternity too.

Notice that this triangle has three points:

- What you really love doing (your passions)
- Your skills and talents (or giftedness)
- God's purposes

Here is a simple equation to help you remember this triangle:

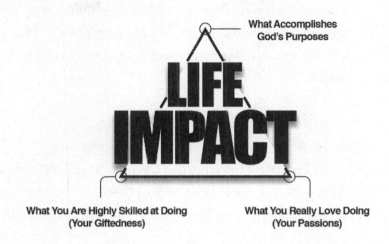

What Accomplishes God's Purposes

LIFE IMPACT

What You Are Highly Skilled at Doing
(Your Giftedness)

What You Really Love Doing
(Your Passions)

Your Passions + Your Gifts + God's Purposes = Your Calling.

What do you love to do?

During a long weekend when my wife and kids are out of town, I always end up in the same place: downstairs on the computer evaluating publicly traded companies and the stock market. For some people this would feel like torture, but for me, it's an absolute joy.

There is something about seeking out the best-performing companies in the world and finding hidden values in the market that exhilarates me. I may start looking at the market at 5:00 p.m., and the next thing I know it's 12:00 a.m. Time passes quickly because studying the stock market is one of my passions.

The first point of the Life Impact Triangle focuses on what you really love doing, or your passions. Maybe you are thinking, *Well, I'm not passionate.* Everyone has a passion for something. You were born with it. Maybe you don't have a passionate personality, but you still have passion. Particular things interest you more than others. These are your passions.

Your passions are your first clue to help you define your personal calling from God and how you can uniquely glorify Him. To understand how you fit into this point of the triangle, ask yourself these questions:

- What do I really enjoy?
- What kind of work or activities do I find rewarding?
- What do I gravitate toward when I have some extra time?
- What activities am I doing when time flies?
- If I could do one thing for the rest of my life, what would it be?
- What would I do if I didn't need to get paid?
- Is there something that someone else I know does that thrills me?
- What have I always dreamed of doing but never gotten to do?
- What did I want to do when I was a child?
- Do I have a dream I have abandoned because I thought it was impractical?
- Is there something I have been afraid to do because it will take me out of my comfort zone?

Sparky Anderson, the legendary baseball manager for the Detroit Tigers and the Cincinnati Reds, once said, "I can't believe they pay us to play baseball—something we did for free as kids."[3] Anderson's comment reveals that having a passion for something is a great motivator to continue doing it, which is why it's important to love what you do.

When you know what you love to do, you'll know what you are passionate about, which means you'll tap into energy to fuel your God-given calling. Without passion, it's difficult to do anything with much endurance—and endurance is definitely needed for any

God-sized calling. Life will also become exciting. Boredom for living will be replaced with anticipation. You will stop feeling like you have to drag yourself out of bed every day just so you can count the days and minutes until the weekend.

In a *Forbes* article titled "8 Reasons Why People Feel Lost in Their Lives," David DiSalvo wrote, "If you're passionate about your main job, that's great. But for many people, their job is a means to pay the bills, not an outlet for their deeply felt passions. But if we always think we're too busy with our jobs and other parts of our daily routines to pursue anything we're passionate about, then feeling incredibly bland, if not lost, is inevitable. I'm a firm believer that every schedule needs some time carved away for passionate pursuits . . . If you're always too busy for passion, the proverbial 'rut' awaits you."[4]

I agree! Remember when I was miserable sitting by the pool during my early retirement, but was energized when I found my way back into business? I was energized because I was living out of my passions. When I wasn't, I felt as though I was stuck in the rut DiSalvo described.

What are your gifts and skills?

In his book *The Element*, Sir Ken Robinson tells a story about a six-year-old boy named Bart who loved to walk on his hands. No one knew why, but it was so easy for him that people said he could walk on his hands just as well as he could on his feet.

His classmates often asked him to demonstrate his trick, and each time he happily popped into a handstand and began walking around on his hands. Eventually Bart could even walk up and down the stairs on his hands—and he loved it.

One day, Bart's physical education teacher got permission from his parents to take him on a field trip to a fully equipped training center for gymnastics. As he walked in, Bart was amazed.

In the book, Robinson wrote, "He'd never seen anything so wondrous in his life. There were ropes, parallel bars, trapezes, ladders, trampolines, hurdles—all kinds of things upon which he could climb, cavort, and swing. It was like visiting Santa's workshop and Disneyland at the same time. It was the ideal place for him. His life turned in that moment. Suddenly his innate skills were good for something more than amusing himself and others."[5]

In the years that followed, Bart Conner trained hard and in 1976 he became a household name in the Montreal Olympics as a gymnast for the United States. He also represented the United States in 1980 and 1984. Bart became the most decorated male American gymnast in history and was inducted into every major Hall of Fame for his sport.

Maybe it seems like a huge disconnect between gymnastics and glorifying God, but every passion, gift, and talent can be used as a platform to glorify Him. A first step is identifying what you love to do because discovering your calling begins by tapping into the deepest longings and the greatest passions of your heart.

I recently heard a story of a professional golfer who leverages his time on the green as an evangelist to glorify God. He strategically writes scriptures on his golf balls in hopes that when other golfers retrieve them, they notice the verses and make comments. This provides him with an open door to talk about his Lord. He has turned golf into an evangelism tool. Not only is this man doing what he loves to do, he is combining it with his love for his Savior.

Can you imagine what even greater things this man could do for God if he taught other golfers to do the same? What if he started a nationwide club for golfers interested in sharing the gospel with others? God can use every passion, gift, and skill for His kingdom. He won't waste a thing if we will give Him everything.

Here are some good questions to get you thinking about your gifts and skills:

- Are you athletic?
- Are you analytical?
- Are you a strategic thinker?
- Are you good at building things?
- Are you skilled in math and science?
- Are you strong in language and verbal skills?
- Are you a "big-picture" person, or do you like project details?
- Are you an articulate speaker?
- Can you make people laugh?
- Do you play a musical instrument well?
- Can you paint?
- Do you like large crowds or small groups?
- Do you prefer to network at a large party or to have a personal conversation in a coffee shop?
- What can you do well with little effort that others have to struggle or expend large amounts of energy to do?
- Do your friends call on you in times of trouble to provide insight?
- Do people seek you out to have fun?
- Do people seek you out to talk?
- Do people seek you out to make a business decision?
- Do people seek you out to grieve over the loss of a loved one?
- Do people seek you out to help them with their kids?
- Do people seek you out to help build or fix things?
- At what times do people want your involvement?

These questions can help point you toward your God-given calling.

What will accomplish God's purposes?

Do you remember that in the first chapter I said that your Blueprint for Life will help you understand what God cares about? What He cares about can also be defined as His purposes.

Throughout Scripture, Jesus has commanded us to evangelize—or tell others about Him—such as in Mark 16:15, "Go into all the world and preach the good news to all creation" (NIV). There are also numerous scriptures that show that we are to care for the poor and needy, such as 1 Timothy 5:3, which indicates that we are to care for widows. Jesus has also said that we should teach others how to follow Him. This is called discipleship. These are three main purposes God wants to accomplish in the world: evangelization, caring for the poor and needy, and for others to follow Him through discipleship.

For more than thirteen years, Tom has worked each summer as a director for Royal Family Kids' Camp, an international organization dedicated to ministering to abused and neglected children. Tom's nine-to-five job is as an electrical engineer, but his God-given calling is to show Jesus' love to underprivileged kids each summer at RFKC in the Idaho mountains.

Every June, kids who have been referred to RFKC through the state Department of Health and Welfare load onto a bus and arrive at camp with hugs, hollers, and cheers from the camp staff.

Sarah, a six-year-old who bounced in and out of fourteen foster homes in twelve months, finally understood RFKC's goal after her third year at camp. "It's about love," she said. Indeed it is. Because many of the campers come from low-income families, birthday gifts are a privilege that many can't afford, so each child receives a box of birthday surprises.

Tom said, "I never realized how some kids have never had something like the items that we see in dollar stores, like pencils and barrettes. Some of them get so excited This year, one seven-year-old boy yelled, 'Look at what God gave me.' We've had foster parents say, 'This is the best thing that happens to these kids all year.' Some of them even start packing for camp in January."[6]

Through RFKC, Tom is pursuing his personal calling to fulfill God's purposes in the world. Your calling may be to finance groups that evangelize, write discipleship materials, or start an organization that uses the Internet to spread God's Word to millions. Whatever your personal calling, it needs to help accomplish God's purposes in the world.

Your Calling May Be the Same— or Different—Than Your Career

After my stint in ministry and by the pool, I met Eric Swartz, who became my partner in a new investment banking firm. On the first day we opened our doors, Eric and I decided to develop a giving fund. We made a commitment to give the first ten cents of every dollar we earned in revenue to a charitable cause or ministry in need. We also started a nonprofit called Ministry Ventures. Since its beginning in 1999, Ministry Ventures has launched more than sixty faith-based organizations to support God's work all over the world.

Through my career as an investment banker, I am helping God fulfill His purposes in the world, which is why I am so passionate about my career. If I was using my gifts and talents only to make money, I would be unsatisfied and miserable. True fulfillment doesn't come from just using one's gifts and talents. True fulfillment comes from using your gifts and talents for something much bigger than yourself.

God has created some men to be cameramen, some to work as advocates for pro-life organizations, and some to be missionaries and pastors. But as I mentioned, He created me to be a businessman. Because this is how I have been designed, this is how I can best glorify Him to experience maximum fulfillment and joy in my life—and to make an eternal impact.

Unlike me, perhaps your career and God-given calling are identical. For example, maybe you are a pastor, so your career and calling are the same. Or maybe your story is more like mine, with a career that supports your God-given calling. Tragically, a lot of people make the error of sacrificing their calling on the altar of their career. They live for this present world and for what their career can give them, such as more money, comfort, or status. As a result, their career hinders their God-given calling, and the people God could touch through them become spiritual casualties of selfishness. Remember that your career or job must always support—and never hinder— your calling to help fulfill God's purposes in the world.

Be bold in pursuing all points of the Life Impact Triangle. When your passions, gifts, and God's purposes align, that is when you can make a big impact for eternity. There is certainly nothing better than that!

ETERNAL PERSPECTIVE SCRIPTURE

"And behold, I am coming quickly, and My reward is with Me, to give to every one according to his work" (Rev. 22:12).

Chapter Four

BEFORE YOU TAKE YOUR FIRST STEPS

S OME OF US LOVE MORNINGS. We hop out of bed with a smile on our face and a bounce in our step. This reminds me of how people may respond when they realize they are passionate about a particular calling and that God has given them unique gifts. They immediately wake up to the idea and are excited about it. They have a bounce in their step and are ready to go! Others slowly wake to the idea that it is possible to pursue their God-given calling.

Regardless of how you begin the pursuit of your calling, there are some additional things you'll need to know before you take your first steps.

EVERYONE STARTS SMALL

Maybe you feel like you are relatively good at many things but not really gifted at anything. If this is how you feel, first take a look at your passions. Sometimes before our gifts are developed, passion is the only thing pointing to a personal calling. In fact, it's even possible to not be aware that you are good at something until you step out and exercise that gift. Be encouraged: gifts and talents are like little seeds. Like a plant, they have to be "watered" to grow—and you water them by using them.

This is where courage comes in. Some people refuse to risk because it is uncomfortable. I think this is where many, many people miss their calling. God has planted a little seed inside of them,

YOUR BLUEPRINT FOR LIFE

so He calls them out: "Psssst, child! I want you to preach for Me."
But because they allow fear to bully them, they decide they can't do
it before they have even tried. Remember, every tree grows from a
seed. Expect small beginnings in your calling.

On his website, John Maxwell shares Leonard Ravenhill's story
of a group of tourists who visited a village in Europe. One of the
tourists asked an elderly villager, "Have any great men been born in
this village?" The old man replied, "Nope, only babies."[1]

No one starts out fulfilling their calling; everyone *grows* into their
calling. In our society, many people think that becoming excellent
at something happens instantly. We forget that every gift starts as a
seed, and all great men—and women—start as babies! Remembering
this will help manage your expectations so you don't get discouraged
or overlook small opportunities that will lead to progress in your
calling later.

Imagine a young, ambitious piano player who dreams of performing before thousands in the world's finest music halls. He knows
this is God's calling for his life, so he envisions lifting his audiences
to heights of auditory rapture as he romances the piano keys.

But when he is asked to play at weddings or at the mall he says,
"Nah, I am going to be a great pianist. I play for thousands, not for
shoppers at the mall or at weddings." He turns down small opportunities God brings his way and fails to see that these offers are not
unimportant. They are bricks that will build the road to becoming
a great pianist.

This young man needs to remember that most people don't
achieve the fullness of their calling overnight. Instead, pursuing
one's calling takes time and persistence. You have to take advantage
of the little opportunities to get to big opportunities later.

Zechariah 4:10 says, "For who has despised the day of small things?" The day of small beginnings happens for everyone—and it's *very good and necessary*. It keeps us humble and dependent on God, and it reminds us that we aren't the god of our own lives. It also prepares us internally for how God wants to use us in the future.

SOMETIMES YOU HAVE TO CREATE YOUR OWN OPPORTUNITY

One of the biggest problems people have is with opportunity. They think, *Well, I know what I want to do, and I know what my gifts are; I know what I am passionate about, but I don't have the opportunities to do what I'd like to do.* This is where a lot of people get stuck.

In a video titled *Why Work Matters*, Pastor Tim Keller said that some people fall into their calling when an opportunity presents itself.[2] For example, someone comes to them and says, "Hey, do you want to launch a new business with me?" Or, "I would like to hire you to work in my office as an office manager." Once they have taken advantage of the opportunity, they find that they like it and realize God has called them to a particular task. They fall into their calling through an open door of opportunity.

Other people are more deliberate. They create an opportunity to pursue their desired calling. For example, Steven, a young man with a passion to educate Christian nonprofits about best marketing practices, is also a skilled writer. He got the idea to start blogging about marketing, and what started out as a small idea has turned into a business. Steven even does seminars and has created a weekly podcast. Some people fall into their calling; others take an active part in pursuing it.

In 1999, I cofounded Ministry Ventures with Boyd Bailey. This powerful organization helps empower ministry leaders by teaching them about best practices for fund-raising, board development, prayer, and administration.

Since its inception, Ministry Ventures has trained approximately one thousand faith-based nonprofits and coached for more than two hundred ministries. By God's grace more than $100 million has been raised through the ministries served and thousands of people have been led into a growing relationship with Jesus Christ.

At the time the organization started, Boyd worked as a director for Crown Financial Ministries but later felt called to work full-time with Ministry Ventures as the organization's chief encouragement officer (CEO). Later, he felt God was calling him to write devotionals, and he currently has more than 105,000 subscribers on his e-mail list. At each juncture of change, when Boyd felt God had called him to take a new step, he didn't wait around. He took action.

Many people wrongly believe if God is calling them to a particular task they shouldn't have to create an opportunity, that He will write it in their Cheerios, strike them with lightning, or speak from heaven in a loud voice telling them that this is His plan. But let me ask this: Could it be that your passions and gifts *are God's green light* to step out in faith and pursue your calling? Could it be that your desire is a sign of His permission for you to move forward in your calling?

When Nehemiah felt a passionate burden to rebuild the wall of Jerusalem, he didn't sit around and wait for someone to ask him to start the task. All he had was a burning inside him for this God-given calling. So he prayed, then he stepped out in faith. He took one step, then another, then another. And each step of the way, God confirmed Nehemiah's calling.

When Corrie ten Boom, a Dutch woman and a former Ravensbrück concentration camp victim, felt God wanted her to become a missionary to the United States, she didn't sit around and wait for someone to invite her onto a mission field. She prayed, then she took the small amount of money she had, booked a flight, and headed abroad. That first step led her to eventually minister to millions through writing and speaking about God's redeeming and forgiving love.

Maybe it's time for you to take a first step toward your calling by creating an opportunity. To start, begin in prayer like Nehemiah. Ask God to guide you. Commit to stay open to His leading as you move forward. Next, make a plan of things you can do to move in the direction of your desired calling.

At first, you may just complete small tasks such as making a phone call that will help you move forward. For example, if you want to become a teacher, you may decide to observe a talented educator in action, become a teacher's aide, or take college classes. The point is, do something! As you move forward and stay sensitive to God's leading, He will guide you. Don't let fear or uncertainty stop you from making progress. It may mean making some radical changes like moving to an unfamiliar city, taking a job that will point you in the right direction, or developing friendships with a new group of people.

Remember, even if it turns out you are wrong about the calling you thought you should pursue, you can never get out of God's hand. The Lord will "perfect" that which concerns you (Ps. 138:8). Stay in communication with Him; your calling will unfold within the context of intimate relationship with Christ.

God Won't Waste a Thing
in Your Calling

You might be saying, "I have so much against me. I can't pursue my calling." "I grew up in a horrible family." "I was abused." "I don't have any money." "I am single." "I am divorced." Or, "I am too young." There are many reasons why we can each feel that we can't pursue our calling.

Be encouraged. God doesn't waste a thing. Your inadequacies and your history will both be leveraged by God as powerful components that will work in your favor to complete your calling.

Who better to work with abused children than someone who has been abused? Who could be more powerful in helping the poor and needy than one who has been poor and needy? Who can provide better comfort for the grieving than the one who has grieved? God will weave your history and even the things that you consider to be inadequacies into your calling.

Rick Jackson of Atlanta is well acquainted with the challenges of being an orphan. Born into a dysfunctional family, he was placed in foster care at the age of thirteen. Thankfully, with God's help, Rick was able to overcome his difficulties and is now a successful entrepreneur. Over the past thirty years Rick has been instrumental in conceptualizing and developing more than twenty-five health-care–related companies, one of which is the third-largest health-care staffing company in the United States.

Rick's experience as an orphan has not been wasted. Instead, God has used it to inspire him to financially support and found Faithbridge, a foster care ministry that has the goal of finding, developing, and training a Christian family for every orphan in America. God is in the business of weaving our history into our calling.

In 2 Corinthians 12:1–4, the apostle Paul wrote about some

special revelations that God gave him of heaven in which he "was caught up to paradise and heard inexpressible things, things that no one is permitted to tell" (UPDATED NIV). Then in verse 7, he added, "To keep me from becoming conceited, I was given a thorn in my flesh, a messenger of Satan, to torment me."

There are different ideas about what his ailment was. But no matter what it was, God used this "thorn in the flesh" to keep Paul humble so that he could more effectively complete his calling. Even in Paul's life, God used what could have been a hindrance as a positive part of Paul's calling.

YOUR CALLING MAY NOT BE WHAT YOU THINK

I like movies when the good guy is successful in his calling. For example, in *The Lord of the Rings*, Frodo miraculously succeeds in destroying the One Ring. In *Apollo 13*, a mission gone awry is completed with a daring and thrilling journey back to the safety of earth. And in the movie *Rudy*, the protagonist overcomes multiple obstacles to fulfill his dream to play football for the University of Notre Dame. I like these films because I love it when a calling is accomplished in glory.

When I think about a calling completed in glory, could there be anything more absurd than the cross? Nothing seems more "anti-glory" than God coming to earth to save His creation from sin by allowing Himself to be murdered. It's definitely not how we would have written God's script. If it were up to us, we'd craft His story like a Hollywood movie. We'd blow up the bad guys, shoot lightning from heaven, and descend in a cloud of fire.

Even the Jews would have rewritten Jesus' script. They expected a Warrior-Messiah coming to save them from their oppressors. But that is not how Christ served up salvation. He did it much differently—and we shouldn't be surprised. After all, Isaiah 55:8 says, "For My thoughts are not your thoughts, nor are your ways My ways."

According to Isaiah, Christ's calling was consistent with God's character of being upside-down from the world's ways. Therefore, because Jesus' calling was accomplished in an unlikely way, it makes sense that our personal callings may be accomplished using unlikely methods too. God may ask you to use your passions and gifts in ways and situations you wouldn't expect.

Take John the Baptist for example. He was Jesus' public relations guy. The Bible says God assigned him the specific calling to put the spotlight on Christ (John 1:6–8). Because this is what he was created for, he did it very well. One day when he saw Jesus coming, he proclaimed, "Look, [everybody!] the Lamb of God, who takes away the sin of the world!" (John 1:29 NIV).

Being the PR guy for God sounds like an awesome assignment, but if you have read all of John's story, you know that God reserves the right to use us in our calling how He chooses.

After John the Baptist spent years pointing others to Christ, John was arrested, thrown into prison, and beheaded. To the natural mind this seems unfair. But remember, your calling is all about Him. You are the clay; He is the potter (Isa. 64:8). You have been bought with a price (1 Cor. 6:20). In John 13:16 Jesus said, "Most assuredly, I say to you, a servant is not greater than his master; nor is he who is sent greater than he who sent him." He has the right to use your passions and gifts through your calling how He chooses. And that way may not make sense.

Don't get me wrong. I am not saying that you will be martyred, although Christians around the world die every day for their faith. I am saying your calling may not play out in your life how you think. God may use your passions and gifts in ways you never imagined. This is why it's important to remain prayerful and stay open to His leading.

Here are two additional ways calling may not play out the way you anticipate.

Your calling involves grace.

Margo is frustrated. She thinks, *Why do some people seem to have it so easy? Their callings seem to unfold without effort for them. I have a friend who was just promoted in her calling and has everything she has ever dreamed of. Why can't that be me? It seems that the harder I work, the harder it gets. I just want to be a successful Christian singer. Is that too much to ask? I want to serve God!*

Margo needs to remember 1 Peter 4:10, which says, "As each one [each person in the body of Christ] has received a gift, minister it to one another, as good stewards of the manifold grace of God."

This scripture says we have *each* been given a gift. Margo doesn't have her friend's, and her friend doesn't have hers. If Margo doesn't have the ability to fulfill a particular calling, it's because God has not graced her for it. She has not received that particular gift.

She also needs to keep in mind that because God has given everyone a gift, everyone has a place to plow in God's field to fulfill His purposes. We are all a part of a body, and no part is insignificant. "But now God has set the members, each one of them, in the body just as He pleased" (1 Cor. 12:18). Some people are given a bigger patch of ground to work than others, but that doesn't mean the smaller or less-noticeable gifts or callings are unimportant.

We have all been given gifts and talents according to our ability. Some people are called to work behind the scenes while some people are called to work out front, but all callings are important to fulfill God's purposes in the world. Success in God's eyes is when we are obedient to the calling that He has given us.

In a parable Jesus told in Matthew 25:14–46, each of three servants was given some talents (money) by their master. The first guy was given five talents, the second one was given two, and the last guy was given one. Each was given talents "according to his own ability" (v. 15) to steward for the master while he was away.

Sometimes we feel like the man who received one talent and we become envious of others, wishing we had their talents. We feel they have more opportunities to make a difference and more influence to fulfill a bigger calling. But we have to remember that we have each been given the gift we have been given by the Lord in accordance with the ability that has been bestowed on us. He has equipped us for what He has called us to.

If God calls a woman to be a singer for the opera and to use her earnings from her profession to support African missions, He will give her the grace and ability to fulfill this calling. If she wants to be an Olympic archery champion and this is not His calling for her, He will not grace her to fulfill it; but someone else will be an archery champion. It's unwise to compare our passions, gifts, and calling to others'. If you do, you will be miserable. Comparison is the enemy of joy. God made you in a particular way, to fulfill a particular role in the body of Christ to glorify Him.

Your calling may be bigger than you.

Even though God has perfectly created you for your personal calling, there will be times when you feel totally unequipped. There will be moments or seasons when you will feel stretched; your calling will be "bigger than you."

Sometimes your calling will be bigger than you because you have a larger-than-life dream that God has placed in your heart, and you know you can't complete it without Him. Other times, He may strategically thrust you into a calling to glorify Him, and you know you will fail without His help. Either way, your calling won't be easy.

When God called Joshua to make the walls of Jericho fall down, there was no way that he could accomplish this task in his own strength. Joshua used his gifts and talents, but he was stretched far beyond his own strength and resources because he needed God's power to succeed. This is why God was glorified when the walls came tumbling down. Joshua couldn't take credit.

When God put it in Nehemiah's heart to rebuild the wall of Jerusalem, he didn't have the supplies he needed. He had the God-given passion, gifts, and talents to do the job. He was a bold leader and strategist. But just like Joshua, Nehemiah couldn't accomplish his calling without God's help. God had to give Nehemiah favor with King Artaxerxes to accomplish the task because it was "bigger than" Nehemiah.

When God told Moses that He was sending him to speak to Pharaoh to convince him to let the Israelites go, Moses felt incapable. He said, "O Lord, I have never been eloquent, neither in the past nor since you have spoken to your servant. I am slow of speech and tongue" (Ex. 4:10 NIV). Moses asked God to send someone else in his place. As a result, God sent Aaron with Moses to speak for him. Even though Moses felt inadequate, it didn't stop God from using him. And just like Joshua and Nehemiah, he needed God to show up because Moses' calling was "bigger than" him.

The world tells you that you have to be in control of all aspects of your calling and you shouldn't admit a need for help. This is not God's way. Even Jesus leaned into His Father as He pressed into

His calling. Psalm 147:10 says, "His pleasure is not in the strength of the horse, nor his delight in the legs of a man; the LORD delights in those who fear [revere] him, who put their hope in his unfailing love" (NIV). And Zechariah 4:6 says, "'Not by might nor by power, but by My Spirit,' says the LORD."

When God wants to demonstrate His glory and make His name great, He isn't looking for the most capable person or the one who believes they are self-sufficient. He is looking for the person who is willing to use what He has placed in their hand to partner with Him to accomplish what seems impossible.

Tragically, most of us dream far too small. We often only want to do for God what we can control and accomplish in our own strength with the resources we already possess. Dream big for God and remember this: what you can do in your own strength is only the beginning of how God can use you for His glory. Can you imagine what He could do through you if you pursued what could only be accomplished with God as your partner?

YOUR CALLING MAY TAKE YOU
OUTSIDE YOUR COMFORT ZONE

I mentioned that after I graduated from college, I entered the workforce as an aerospace engineer. My parents were proud, and I was glad to have my new diploma in hand. But from the very first day at my new job I knew I was going to be miserable. Little stimulation. No creativity. Stuck in a little grey box crunching numbers. I quickly discovered that engineering wasn't for me. So after three years, I traded my secure income at my aerospace engineering job to become a copier salesman.

One day I was designing jet fighters, and the next day I was pulling a copier down the street and getting doors slammed in my face. When I called my mom and dad to tell them about my new position, they were shocked. "How could you throw five years of engineering school down the drain to sell copiers?'

I knew they wouldn't understand, but I had a deep-down feeling I was made for something more. I knew God had created me with other passions and gifts. If I wanted to be all that He had called me to be, I had to trade what was comfortable for what was uncomfortable.

There were some drawbacks to the job. One, I was working straight commission. That meant I wasn't sure if I would get a paycheck anytime soon. Two, I had to load up a van full of copiers each morning at 8:00 a.m. in a suit and tie in muggy West Palm Beach, Florida. Three, each day I was required to make fifty walk-in cold calls—before lunch.

Most of my prospects kicked me out within five seconds of walking into their office. The rejection was unbearable. At the end of my first day on the job, I sat in my van and sobbed.

After the first month or two, with tears and fears behind me, I started to make some sales and actually became one of the top copier salesmen in South Florida.

As word got out to management that there was an engineering guy who could actually sell, I got a phone call from the parent company. It just so happened that the parent company was a two-billion-dollar defense contractor and was looking for engineers with sales experience to market their products to the Pentagon. To make a long story short, I landed a job with Harris Corporation and was on my way to a successful career as a businessman.

What I didn't realize at the time is that my decision to leave my engineering job turned out to be a pivotal point in my career and central to my unfolding calling. If I had never made the choice to get outside my "aerospace-engineer" box, I wouldn't be where I am today, leveraging my career to support my personal calling to financially support and launch Christian organizations that are making Jesus famous.

If you refuse to be uncomfortable, your calling will be limited by your current level of comfort. At every step of your journey when you want to make more impact for God, you will need faith—and that sometimes means stepping into the unknown. You can't fulfill your personal calling without risk, just like you can't fulfill it without having an eternal perspective, which is the third step to creating your Blueprint for Life.

ETERNAL PERSPECTIVE SCRIPTURE

God "will render to each one according to his deeds" (Rom. 2:6).

Chapter Five

TO INFINITY AND BEYOND

IMAGINE THAT NASA IS SO impressed with your first space voyage that they invite you on another unique trip. But this one is going to be longer because the engineers at Space Command have developed a way to leverage the speed of light so you can travel forever and never die. To get this "anti-aging effect," you will have to zip around Betelgeuse, Alpha Centauri, and in and out of the Milky Way and the other one hundred million galaxies without ever stopping. The thought of never dying thrills you, so you suit up, take a deep breath, step into your rocket, and start your forever journey.

TIME IS SHORT AND ETERNITY IS LONG

It's hard to imagine zipping around the planets forever because everything in our world has an expiration date. The milk in your refrigerator has an expiration date, your car registration has an expiration date, and even your body has an expiration date. You may have heard people say, "Nothing lasts forever." Well, nothing *on earth* lasts forever.

But three things *will* last forever: God's Word, eternity—and you.

One day your breath will return to God and you will meet your Maker. In the very moment that you pass from earth to heaven, the opportunities you had to use your passions, gifts, and calling to glorify Christ will be finished. But the good news is that in eternity you will receive rewards from Christ for how you served Him while on the earth.

In a delightful reflection titled "To Remember Me" in an edition of *Chicken Soup for the Soul*, Robert N. Test describes how the day will come when he will lie upon a white sheet on a hospital bed and a doctor will declare that he has died. Test charges those who care for him not to attempt to keep him alive using artificial methods. He also does not want anyone to call this final bed his deathbed because he considers it his "Bed of Life."

He calls it his Bed of Life because he will give all that he is to those he leaves behind. He will give his sight to a man who has never seen a sunrise, his heart to someone who has only known pain. He will give his blood to a teen who was torn from the wreckage of a car, so that he may see his grandchildren play. And, he will give his kidneys, his bones, every muscle, fiber, and nerve his body to help a crippled child walk. He will also give his brain and his cells so they may grow to help a deaf child hear. Finally, he writes:

> Burn what is left of me and scatter the ashes to the winds to help the flowers grow. If you must bury something, let it be my faults, my weaknesses and all prejudice against my fellow man.
>
> Give my sins to the devil. Give my soul to God.
>
> If, by chance, you wish to remember me, do it with a kind deed or word to someone who needs you. If you do all I have asked, I will live forever.[1]

In this reflection, the author celebrates the blessings he will leave behind. For the faithful Christian who has served Christ well, they can celebrate the truth of the good works they did on the earth, but also celebrate that their good works will follow them to heaven.

Some people have never heard of the doctrine of eternal rewards, and when they do, they get salvation and rewards confused. Let me be clear: salvation has nothing to do with rewards. We are saved by grace and Christ's blood sacrifice on the cross for our sins, but God promises we will be rewarded in heaven for what we have done on the earth.

In a message titled "The Doctrine of Eternal Rewards," Randy Alcorn said, "The doctrine of eternal rewards hinges on specific acts of faithfulness done on Earth that survive the believer's judgment and are brought into Heaven with us" (1 Cor. 3:14).[2]

There are numerous scriptures on eternal rewards, but here are just a few of my favorites . . .

- Behold, I am coming quickly, and My reward is with Me, to give to every one according to his work. (Rev. 22:12)
- For we must all appear before the judgment seat of Christ, so that each of us may receive what is due us for the things done while in the body, whether good or bad. (2 Cor. 5:10 NIV)
- Do not lay up for yourselves treasures on earth, where moth and rust destroy and where thieves break in and steal; but lay up for yourselves treasures in heaven. (Matt. 6:19–20.)

Understanding and believing these scriptures and embracing the truth about eternal rewards is transforming. It brings clarity and purpose to life and great conviction about how lasting the impact of loving God and glorifying Him truly is.

In her book *Heaven: Your Real Home*, Joni Eareckson Tada wrote:

When a Christian realizes his citizenship is in heaven, he begins acting as a responsible citizen of earth. He invests wisely in relationships because he knows they're eternal. His conversations, goals, and motives become pure and honest because he realizes these will have bearing on everlasting reward. He gives generously of time, money, and talent because he's laying up treasure for eternity. He spreads the good news of Christ because he longs to fill heaven's ranks with his friends and neighbors. All this serves the pilgrim well not only in heaven, but on earth; for it serves everyone around him.[3]

As Joni said, understanding and believing in eternal rewards will affect every area of your life—including how you use your gifts and calling. You will start to see that you haven't just been called to accept Christ as Lord, but you have been called to demonstrate your love for Him through action.

Maybe you are wondering what we will specifically be rewarded for when we get to heaven and what it means to live a life of value. To begin to answer that question, let's take a look at a story from Scarlett O'Hara.

HEAVENLY REWARDS

When Union soldiers burned Atlanta and overturned Tara in the film *Gone with the Wind*, Scarlett O'Hara was frantic. Her family had lost everything. Her father was trying to cope with the devastation of the South and had slipped into a mild dementia. Scarlett just wanted a normal life again on the plantation but was running out of options. Then she noticed a stack of Confederate bonds her father had been saving for a rainy day.

"Oh, Pa . . . what are those papers?" Scarlett asked.

"Bonds," he replied. "They're all we've saved. All we have left. Bonds."

"But what kind of bonds, Pa?"

"Why, Confederate bonds of course, darling."

"Confederate bonds," Scarlett lamented. "What good are they to anybody?"[4]

Society tells us we can live a life of value; but we have to drive the right kind of car, make more money, live in a bigger house, have a better body, or get a better tan. And unfortunately, lots of times we believe the lies. So, we spend our lives—just like Scarlett's father—investing our days in that which will lose its value after we go home to heaven.

A life of value is defined by those things that will make a difference in eternity. This includes how you glorify God by living out your calling. Nothing else will matter after you die. If it doesn't make a difference in heaven, it's not worth pursuing on earth. When you stand before Christ, He won't ask you if you had a six-figure income, because that has no value in heaven. He won't ask you if you drove a hot car, or were an executive at your company, because those things won't matter in heaven. He won't ask you if you followed the latest fashions, because after you die, it just won't matter if you looked stylish.

Instead, He will want to know if you followed Him, obeyed Him, lived your life according to His will, and used your passions and gifts to make Him great and accomplish His purposes in the world.

If we want to invest our lives in what truly matters, a good place to start is by comparing what the world values with what God values. For example . . .

The world says, "Be the top dog! The one who is worshipped wins."

But God's Word says, "If anyone desires to be first, he shall be last of all and servant of all" (Mark 9:35).

The world says, "Repay those who hurt you."

God's Word says, "Do not repay anyone evil for evil" (Rom. 12:17 NIV).

The world says, "Look out for number one."

God's Word says, "If anyone would come after me, he must deny himself and take up his cross daily and follow me" (Luke 9:23 NIV).

The world says, "Get all you can and keep everything for yourself."

God's Word says, "Give to the one who asks you, and do not turn away from the one who wants to borrow from you" (Matt. 5:42 NIV).

The world says, "Make friends with influential people for self-promotion."

God's Word says, "Do nothing out of selfish ambition or vain conceit, but in humility consider others better than yourselves. Each of you should look not only to your own interests, but also to the interests of others" (Phil. 2:3–4 NIV).

The world says, "The one who dies with the most toys wins."

God's Word says, "Watch out! Be on your guard against all kinds of greed; a man's life does not consist in the abundance of his possessions" (Luke 12:15 NIV).

The world says, "It's all about me."

God's Word says, "It's all about Me."

If you want to make an eternal impact for Christ, you will have to go against the world's ways to love and glorify Christ. That means you'll have to change your definition of what is valuable.

God Rewards What God Values

When you were growing up, did your parents say, "If you get an A, I'll give you a dollar"? If so, then you could tell what they valued by what they rewarded. It's the same way with God. You can tell what He values by what He rewards. Here are a few specific things God will reward His servants for . . .

Faithful Service to Christ as Master
In Matthew 24:45–47 Jesus said, "Who then is a faithful and wise servant, whom his master made ruler over his household, to give them food in due season? Blessed is that servant whom his master, when he comes, will find so doing. Assuredly, I say to you that he will make him ruler over all his goods."

Faithful Service to Your Employer as Unto the Lord
Colossians 3:22–24 says, "Bondservants, obey in all things your masters according to the flesh, not with eyeservice, as men-pleasers, but in sincerity of heart, fearing God. And whatever you do, do it heartily, as to the Lord and not to men, knowing that from the Lord you will receive the reward of the inheritance; for you serve the Lord Christ."

Seeking Him Through Prayer
Matthew 6:6 says, "But you, when you pray, go into your room, and when you have shut your door, pray to your Father who is in the secret place; and your Father who sees in secret will reward you openly."

Serving Those in Need in His Name
In Mark 9:41 Jesus says, "For whoever gives you a cup of water to

drink in My name, because you belong to Christ, assuredly, I say to you, he will by no means lose his reward."

Suffering for His Name and Reputation

In Luke 6:22–23, Jesus said, "Blessed are you when men hate you, and when they exclude you, and revile you, and cast out your name as evil, for the Son of Man's sake. Rejoice in that day and leap for joy! For indeed your reward is great in heaven, for in like manner their fathers did to the prophets."

Sacrificing for Him

In Luke 6:35 Jesus said, "But love your enemies, do good, and lend, hoping for nothing in return; and your reward will be great, and you will be sons of the Most High. For He is kind to the unthankful and evil."

Sharing Your Time, Talent, and Treasure to Further His Kingdom

In Matthew 6:3–4, Jesus said, "But when you do a charitable deed, do not let your left hand know what your right hand is doing, that your charitable deed may be in secret; and your Father who sees in secret will Himself reward you openly."

In 1 Timothy 6:18–19 Paul also wrote, "Let them do good, that they be rich in good works, ready to give, willing to share, storing up for themselves a good foundation for the time to come, that they may lay hold on eternal life."

These "good works" Paul described include how you serve Him using your passions, gifts, and calling.

John Bevere wrote about his determination to make his life count for Christ in his book *Driven by Eternity*.

I recall when I was saved in my college fraternity at Purdue University. I immediately started seeking God's desire for my life. I was a student of engineering and worked every other semester at IBM. One of the reasons that motivated me to know my calling, other than just desiring to obey God, was that just a few months after being saved I was in an office with a group of eight to ten engineers celebrating a man's thirty-eighth year of service. We were casually chatting and this man said to all of us, "I've hated coming to this job every day for thirty-eight years." Everyone else in the room either agreed or snickered, except me; I was in shock.

As a rookie among seasoned professionals, I wondered why no one else commented differently, so I blurted out, "Why have you done this for thirty-eight years if you've hated it?"

He looked back at me and said, "It's a job."

I, too, had found myself having an aversion to coming in. My dad was an engineer, and he said it was a good profession that was secure and paid well. But this encounter caused me to change my outlook. I thought, *No money, security, or anything else is going to keep me from my reason for being placed on earth.* I made up my mind right there that I would find out what I was called to do and what the next step was that I needed to take to move toward it . . .

The more I sought God, the more I felt drawn to ministry. I didn't like the sounds of that either, but I was smart enough to know that in obeying God I would find fulfillment and satisfaction. Once I made the commitment to Him that I would obey no matter what, He began to show me an overall picture of what He had called me to do on the earth.[5]

You will discover what God has called you to as you earnestly seek Him, determining that you will take whatever risks are necessary and that you will not allow criticism, discomfort, or the fear of the unknown stop you. Seek Him. He will show you why He has created you. Don't settle like the man John Bevere described. Instead, decide that you won't let anything keep you from your reason for being placed on the earth. It matters how you steward your life.

OBEDIENCE TO THE CALL

Bevere also wrote how important it is to plan for our eternal future. Of those who plan for forever with God, he said, "They live with purpose and know their eternal destiny is being written by how they live on the earth. This will provide them a grand entrance into the Kingdom of God, rather than them slipping in with all they've done burned up and destroyed."[6]

What? Burned up? Destroyed? What is John talking about? He is referring to 1 Corinthians 3:12–15, which reads: "If any man builds on this foundation [Jesus Christ] using gold, silver, costly stones, wood, hay or straw, his work will be shown for what it is, because the Day [when Jesus Christ returns] will bring it to light. It will be revealed with fire, and the fire will test the quality of each man's work. If what he has built survives, he will receive his reward. If it is burned up, he will suffer loss; he himself will be saved, but only as one escaping through the flames" (NIV).

Building with gold, silver, and costly stones means "building on Christ" by obeying Him and His will—including your calling—for your life. Building with wood, hay, or straw means following your own fleshly desires to live life your own way regardless of God's will.

Can you imagine working your entire life, doing good works

and accomplishing things that you thought would matter to God, then finally meeting Him face-to-face only to realize that you were only doing what sounded good to you and that you weren't "building on Christ" at all?

Granted, no one builds entirely on Christ, because we sin. For this reason, I'm glad salvation does not depend on works (Eph. 2:8–9); instead, we are justified through the blood of Christ (1 Cor. 6:11). But as you can see, heavenly rewards do depend on works, and those rewards will be a direct result of how we lived on the earth. Perhaps these heavenly rewards are a reason why Paul exhorted the Philippians to work out their salvation with fear and trembling (Phil. 2:12).

All of this doesn't mean that if you are a stay-at-home mom that you should feel guilty, thinking to yourself, *I should be doing more for Christ*. Neither does it mean that if you are not in the ministry that you should run out to become a missionary. Instead, remember that God's rewards will be granted based on obedience to fulfill whatever He has called you to, whether you're a doctor, teacher, stay-at-home mom, or landscaper. Therefore, your life's calling must begin and end with Him. So when He reveals what He wants you to do with your life, do it wholeheartedly! Then, when you come into His kingdom, you will hear, "Well done, good and faithful servant" (Matt. 25:21).

Rewards Are Personal

Matthew 16:27 says, "For the Son of Man will come in the glory of His Father with His angels, and then He will reward each according to his works."

Notice that this scripture says that *each* person will be

rewarded according to his works. I won't be rewarded according to your works, and you won't be rewarded for mine. Each of us will be rewarded according to what we have individually done for Christ.

So when we stand before Jesus, we won't be able to look at someone else and blame him or her for what we didn't do. And we won't be able to receive rewards based on someone else's merit. We will *each* be rewarded.

Obeying Christ

Pastor Tony Evans has said, "Success isn't what you've done compared to what others have done. Success is what you've done compared to what you were created to do."[7]

As believers, we can do good things, but if we aren't headed toward God's goals, if they aren't His will, we'll get zero points for eternal rewards; and more importantly, what we do won't have the same eternal impact. It's important to remember that doing good isn't the goal. Knowing Christ, doing His will, and being obedient to Him is the goal so we can glorify Him with our entire lives and make an impact. By keeping our eyes on His will, we make a powerful difference for Him that will matter.

Some people think it's selfish to factor motivation for eternal rewards into our earthly life. I disagree. In fact, Christ *invites* us to store up treasure in heaven (Matt. 6:20) by doing His will. He wants to reward us after we die for participating in the things He cares about. He wants to reward us for building His kingdom.

Psalm 127:1 says, "Unless the Lord builds the house, they labor in vain who build it." We can build apart from the Spirit of God, but our labor will be worthless in eternity. It will all be burned up at the judgment seat of Christ. It is crucial we understand this.

Doing good works—and even fulfilling what we believe is our calling—doesn't guarantee rewards. This is why we can only fulfill our true calling within the context of knowing Christ and being directed by His Spirit. It's only when we stay in relationship with Him that we can bear fruit that lasts.

Don't waste your life on fleeting endeavors that will have no value after your body turns to dust. Instead, use everything you are and everything you have to make a difference for Christ. "He who has My commandments and keeps them, it is he who loves Me. And he who loves Me will be loved by My Father, and I will love him and manifest Myself to him. . . . He who does not love Me does not keep My words; and the word which you hear is not Mine but the Father's who sent Me" (John 14:21, 24).

ETERNAL PERSPECTIVE SCRIPTURE

"Then I heard a voice from heaven saying to me, 'Write: "Blessed are the dead who die in the Lord from now on."' 'Yes,' says the Spirit, 'that they may rest from their labors, and their works follow them'" (Rev. 14:13).

Chapter Six

BUILDING BELIEF

O N MAY 6, 1954, Roger Bannister, a twenty-five-year-old medical student, stepped into the runner's starting blocks at Oxford's Iffley Road track outside London, England. Bannister was running against his old university for the Amateur Athletic Association.

The competition was stiff. But to everyone's surprise, Bannister not only defeated the other runners in his heat, he also surpassed every man in history who had competed in the mile run, because he was the first man to shatter the four-minute mile.

For years, experts thought it was humanly impossible to run a mile in less than four minutes—and decades of races had consistently proven their theory. So naturally, news of Bannister's run shocked the world.

But what happened next was even more amazing.

Less than two months later, Australia's John Landy beat Bannister's world-record time with another sub-four-minute mile. That same year, New Zealand's Peter Snell joined Bannister and Landy, bettering the pace even further. And in the months that followed, dozens more runners joined the sub-four club. It was soon commonplace to break four minutes.

For centuries, four minutes had marked the limit of human achievement, and every man who stepped onto the track bowed submissively to this common preconception. But on May 6, 1954, Bannister shattered the old myth. And in the process, he issued an invitation for runners everywhere to join him. Soon they joined him in droves. Did he introduce a new running style? A special way to train? Dietary secrets? No. Bannister simply contributed the one thing that had been missing all those years: belief. Once they saw it done, they had no choice but to believe it could be done. And if Bannister could do it, so could they.

There is a simple principle in this illustration that applies to everyone who wants to accomplish anything: *belief is foundational for success.*

Bannister's contemporaries were limited by one thing: their level of belief. They desired to break the four-minute mile, and they were clearly capable—but only when they believed it could be done did they succeed. The same principle applies to you. Your level of belief is often the only thing that holds you where you are. This has powerful implications when it comes to pursuing your calling.

Maybe you are thinking, *Wait a minute! This sounds like some positive-thinking message or prosperity gospel.* I understand if you think this way because the concept of believing has been so abused that many Christians shy away from even mentioning it for fear of being misunderstood. But the concept of belief wasn't invented by new-age teachers or preachers of the prosperity gospel. It was created by God and is stated clearly in His Word.

Here are a few scriptures on belief—or what the Bible often refers to as faith.

- And He said to them, "Because of the littleness of your faith; for truly I say to you, if you have faith the size of a mustard seed, you will say to this mountain, 'Move from here to there,' and it will move; and nothing will be impossible to you." (Matt. 17:20 NASB)

- And Jesus answered and said to them, "Truly I say to you, if you have faith and do not doubt, you will not only do what was done to the fig tree, but even if you say to this mountain, 'Be taken up and cast into the sea,' it will happen." (Matt. 21:21 NASB)
- Truly, truly, I say to you, he who believes in Me, the works that I do, he will do also; and greater works than these he will do; because I go to the Father. (John 14:12 NASB)
- Who is he who overcomes the world, but he who believes that Jesus is the Son of God? (1 John 5:5)

Clearly, God isn't here for us; we are here for Him. However, He has given us the ability to create and work for Him, to envision what our lives will be like, and to believe in what is possible for our calling. And, within the context of relationship with Him, the gift of belief is powerful to help build God's kingdom!

In this chapter, I want to help you understand how God created your mind to believe so that you can use your gifts and talents in the best way possible, in the maximum way possible, to glorify Him in the greatest degree possible.

One of Webster's definitions for *belief* is to "accept or regard (something) as true." When I talk about belief, I am not talking about stirring up positive feelings so you believe something is true to manipulate God. Belief should never be used to treat God like a divine vending machine. You need the right motives for believing. Instead, belief should always be exercised to serve Him. It's about doing the good works He created you to accomplish since the foundation of the world (Eph. 2:10); it's about fulfilling His calling for your life to glorify Him.

Also remember that believing doesn't guarantee life will work out just like you want. God made us with certain limits. But please hear this: *those limits usually aren't as confining as the ones we place on ourselves because of a lack of belief.* We have no idea what God might want to do through us until we believe enough to attempt what seems impossible, until we take one step at a time toward our calling. You don't know what potential He has placed inside of you until you attempt to be something that you haven't been!

Unbelief will hold you right where you are.

Please allow me to use the simple example of baking a cake to illustrate this truth.

If I believe that whipping up a chocolate cake is possible, I will develop a plan—or vision—to make it. I might even be passionate about it if it's for a special occasion. When belief is combined with passion and vision, it will create action. It will lead me to bake the cake.

But without belief, I won't even make it to the grocery store to purchase sugar and flour because unbelief *always* stifles action. Without believing something is possible, passion and vision will die and there definitely won't be any forward movement.

Since these truths apply to something as simple as baking a cake, they also apply to other bigger endeavors too, such as building a business, starting an orphanage, pursuing a singing career, or graduating from college.

Kathy Lamancusa shared a story about the power of belief and how it creates vision that creates action in *Condensed Chicken Soup for the Soul*.[1]

When Kathy's son was born with club feet, the doctors said he would never be able to run, even though he would be able to walk. After years of surgery, casts, and braces, Joey could walk normally by the time he was eight years old. He played with the neighbor kids, but Kathy and her husband never told Joey he would probably never be able to run as well as the other kids. So, Joey just didn't know.

In seventh grade, Joey decided to do something that he would have considered impossible, *if* he knew about his condition . . . he decided to go out for the cross-country team. He was dedicated and trained harder than the other kids. He kept running four or five miles a day, every day—even one day when he had a 103-degree fever.

His dad was worried about him, so he went to look for him after school. He found Joey running alone. With two more miles to go, sweat ran down his face. His eyes were glassy from his fever. But Joey kept his eyes fixed on his goal and kept running. Because Joey's parents never told him he couldn't run with a fever, he just didn't know.

Two weeks later, the kids who made the team were announced. Joey was number six on the list. He had made the team! Because his parents never told him he couldn't make the team, he believed that he could.

You might be wondering how you can believe like Joey so you can use your passions and gifts to fulfill His calling for your life.

Here are four ways to build belief:

FOCUS

When I was twenty-six, after I landed my job as a salesman for Harris Corporation, I drove a pea-green Honda Accord that had been handed down to us from my wife's aunt. It had sheepskin seat covers and was such a bomb that if Homeland Security had existed back then, it would have been confiscated to protect the American citizens.

Every morning, I drove my gem of a car to Denny's, where I ordered a cup of coffee and pulled my microcassette recorder out of my briefcase. (If you're too young to remember microcassettes, we used them to do voice recordings before everything went digital!) In these morning moments, every bright goal I had for my future tumbled out of my mind and through my lips to be recorded for recollection later that day in a powerful rendition of my life's future attractions.

First, I *wrote down* what I wanted to happen in my life: who I wanted to become and what I wanted to accomplish. Then I *spoke* what I had written into a microcassette as if I had already reached my goals. "I am a top salesman at a national software company." "I own a business. I am a pilot. I own my own airplane."

Finally, each evening at 6:00 p.m., I *reviewed* what I had written and verbalized earlier in the day when I left work and drove home in my little car the same way I had come and listened to my morning recording. Over the next year and a half, my dreams played back to me over and over, day after day, after I drove to Denny's and recorded my desires.

Five years later, after moving to Atlanta, I was in the basement of my home where I worked to clear out an overstuffed junk closet. While sifting through a pile of papers, I came across an old shoebox filled with my dreams on microcassette.

I dusted off each cassette, refreshed the player with new batteries, and listened to one cassette, then another, then another. I couldn't believe what I was hearing. Events that I could not have manipulated into happening had become reality. Owning a business—a restaurant, in fact. Being the top software salesman in a Fortune 500 company and achieving financial success.

I was no longer driving the pea-green Honda, and I was living out my dreams—but not only my dreams. They were the dreams that God had placed in my heart. I was fulfilling His calling for my life. Being a businessman was—and is—the best way I can use my passions and gifts for His kingdom by supporting Christian ministries, which brings me a lot of joy.

Writing down my goals, *verbalizing* my goals, and finally *reviewing* my goals helped me to focus on them; and in the process my level of belief about what was possible grew. Focusing created momentum to help me reach my goals.

In addition to building belief, focusing does three other things: 1) it increases the likelihood you'll reach your goals; 2) it creates a sticky filter; and 3) it eliminates—or minimizes—distractions.

A Much Greater Likelihood

My son, Carson, loves to hunt. Lately he has been asking, "Dad, will you take me duck hunting?" Let's imagine I say, "Sure, we'll go" but then I walk away, and because life gets busy, I forget what I told him. What do you think the chances are that we'll go duck hunting if he doesn't remind me? Pretty much zero, right?

Now imagine that instead of just saying "Sure, we'll go" I also write, "Take Carson duck hunting" on a bunch of Post-it notes and stick them inside my car and on my bathroom mirror where I can see them each morning. Now, what do you think the chances are that I will take him duck hunting? Of course, they are much higher because I have intentionally focused on going.

This is the main principle of focus: you place at the forefront of your mind what God wants you to do for Him to reach a desired goal. As you focus, your destination will become more prominent in your mind. This is why I tell people, "What you focus on expands." Because God wants you to fulfill His blueprint for your life and He has work for you to do for Him, you can't leave it to chance. You must live intentionally. Focus will exponentially increase the likelihood that you'll reach your goal.

A Sticky Filter

A second benefit of focus is that it creates what I call a "sticky filter."

Let's imagine that Jim decides he would like to start a home improvement company. He writes down this goal for his calling on a Post-it note and sticks it on his bathroom mirror where he can see it each day. He also writes down his goal on a 4x6 card and places it on the dashboard of his car. The following morning, as he is reading a magazine, an article about starting your own business grabs his attention. Later that afternoon he receives an e-mail among the hundreds of others that he gets every day for a class for aspiring entrepreneurs. Intrigued, he opens it.

Two weeks earlier, he wouldn't have given either the magazine or the e-mail a second thought, but now he does because they are related to what he wants to accomplish. For Jim, focus created a "sticky filter." This sticky filter will cause you to notice solutions in your environment, in your conversations, in your thoughts, and in other forms of input that come in through your five senses that will help you reach your desired destination.

This "sticky filter" concept is what marketers use to reach target markets. They know that consumers only "see what they already see." Meaning, products and services only interest people when they are related to something they are already internally focused on. Therefore, they create messaging and build their brand to speak to a particular target group's desires.

A Handle on Distractions

Because focusing creates a "sticky filter," it's not surprising that it eliminates—or reduces—the power of distractions.

In a typical day, thousands of things compete for your attention: television commercials, e-mails, radio advertisements, needs from your family, needs from friends. The list goes on and on. Of course, you can only give your attention to one idea at a time. When you focus on your destination, it will help you overcome the millions of daily distractions to help you achieve your calling and God's overall blueprint for your life.

Focusing is like grasping the steering wheel of your life. Without focus, you will wander aimlessly from one thing to another. You'll be pulled by every good idea that comes your way. But practicing focus will help you stay the course on the way to your desired destination when other conflicting opportunities look interesting.

PRAY

A second way to build belief is through prayer. Through prayer, the Holy Spirit meets us to prepare us for what is to come. It's also our opportunity to pray over God's blueprint for us. During prayer, we may sense that the direction we are going is not the direction God wants us to go and that He is asking us to make adjustments.

In 2013, I felt called to start a new organization called iDisciple (idisciple.org) to deliver great Christian content to people on their mobile devices to encourage them in their walk with Christ. I am confident I am in God's will in this endeavor; it has also demanded belief that God will show up because it is in an industry in which I don't have experience. (I always tell people to choose goals that are so big that God will have to show up to succeed. I have definitely taken my own advice!)

During this season of launching this new ministry, I have consistently prayed for four things:

1. Stamina to go the distance
2. Direction from God to be able to discern His will
3. Resources to accomplish the task
4. Vision to accomplish the task

I encourage you to pray for the above things as well as you pursue your calling.

Prayer and communion with Christ have kept me focused on what God wants me to accomplish for Him, alerted me to changes I need to make, and helped me endure the many obstacles that happen on the road to success. And, it has helped build my belief!

Lots of people pray, but because fear paralyzes them or they don't know where to start, they don't take any steps to start toward their calling. Granted, there are times when God may ask us to wait to begin moving forward, but there will always be a time to act once we have prayed.

ACT

In *Draw the Circle: The 40 Day Prayer Challenge*, author Mark Batterson tells a story about a group of Mississippi farmers who gathered to pray for rain fifty years ago. In this story, not only did one of the farmers pray, but he also put his prayer into action. This is the third way to build belief.

> When a drought threatened to destroy a season of crops, a rural church with many farmers in the congregation called for an emergency prayer meeting. Dozens of farmers showed up to pray. Most of them wore their traditional overalls, but one of them wore waders! He got a few funny looks, just as Noah did when he was building the ark, but isn't that faith at its finest? If we genuinely believe God is going to answer our prayer for rain, isn't that exactly what we would wear? Why not dress for a miracle? I love the simple, childlike faith of that old, seasoned farmer. He simply said, "I don't want to walk home wet." And he didn't. But everyone else did.[2]

When we pray but don't act, we may be saying we believe God, but we are acting as though we don't. Batterson also wrote, "We can pray until our knees are numb, but if our praying isn't accompanied by acting, then we won't get anywhere. We need to put feet to our faith. After kneeling down, then we need to stand up and step out in faith."[3]

When Queen Esther received the call to rescue her people from annihilation, she fasted along with the Jews in Sushan and her maids for three days and three nights. Then she stood up and stepped out in faith with a plan to save her people. Her belief led her to action. She *did something*. She didn't get caught in analysis paralysis or worry too much about messing up so that she didn't act at all. Instead, with boldness she trusted God with the outcome when she approached the king: "And so I will go to the king, which is against the law; and if I perish, I perish!" (Est. 4:16). Esther "put on her waders" by acting in belief after she prayed.

How to act in belief isn't always as difficult as one might think. You just need to take one little step at a time.

Put Down Stepping-Stones

Because your calling will always be progressive, one of the most important skills in the process of fulfilling your calling is the ability to break down your goal into small steps. These are called "stepping-stones." As you reach each stepping-stone, your vision for what's ahead will become clearer, your motivation will skyrocket, and your level of belief will grow! Let me clarify that this doesn't mean the path will always be straight or what you envisioned. In fact, I can guarantee that God will move some stepping-stones as He leads you. But rest assured, He will get you where He wants you to go. So remember that as you focus, you need to focus on one step at a time, keep the bigger picture in mind, and remain flexible to God's leading.

Here's an example of how stepping-stones work:

Imagine you want to become president of the United States. It's something you have aspired to do since you were in third grade. The thought of making your way to the Oval Office could seem overwhelming, unless you break down your calling into small steps.

So you put down your first stepping-stone when you decide to run for president of your homeowner's association. After you have reached this goal, then you go after your next stepping-stone to run for mayor. Then, state representative, congress, and governor. You take one step at a time on the political path until you finally have your shot at president.

You may have heard it said, "If God has called you to it, He will see you through it." It's true. Your job is to cooperate with Him, stay flexible to His leading, but make a plan with stepping-stones!

When you break your goals into smaller steps, you can maintain the confidence necessary to keep your heart in your calling instead of becoming paralyzed by the enormity of it—and your belief will grow!

King David was a great example of growing belief. It may seem to some that his decision to face the giant warrior Goliath was naïve or an uninformed burst of holy indignation. He wasn't trying to impress the teenage girls or vastly underestimating his opponent's size. His confidence and level of belief that it was possible to defeat Goliath was the culmination of belief that grew over time.

Early on in life, David had a strong conviction that God would protect him from any enemies he faced. Perhaps he embraced the idea immediately, or maybe he needed convincing. We don't know for sure. But by the time he faced Goliath, we know he had tested the hypothesis several times. When Saul confronted David with his shortcomings as a warrior, David explained his vision and his faith to the king. Their conversation went like this:

> "Don't be ridiculous!" Saul replied. "How can a kid like you fight with a man like him? You are only a boy, and he has been in the army *since* he was a boy!"
>
> But David persisted. "When I am taking care of my father's sheep," he said, "and a lion or a bear comes and grabs a lamb from the flock, I go after it with a club and take the lamb from its mouth. If it turns on me, I catch it by the jaw and club it to death. I have done this to both lions and bears, and I'll do it to this heathen Philistine too, for he has defied the armies of the living God! The Lord who saved me from the claws and teeth of the lion and the bear will save me from this Philistine!"

Saul finally consented, "All right, go ahead," he said, "and may the Lord be with you!" (1 Sam. 17:33–37 TLB)

Do you see the progression in David's level of belief? First he defeated lions and bears, so now he knew he was ready for a giant named Goliath. This is also the model for stepping-stones. You don't have to do great things to glorify God all at once. You only have to be great one step at a time while your belief grows and your calling is accomplished.

Remember: focus, pray, act, and put down stepping-stones. Then your belief will grow.

In the second half of the book, I want to take a look at the Big Five that support your calling so you can keep your life in balance the way the Architect desires. These are the five spokes of the wheel of your life that create a vehicle to carry out your God-given calling.

ETERNAL PERSPECTIVE SCRIPTURE

"For we must all appear before the judgment seat of Christ, that each one may receive the things done in the body, according to what he has done, whether good or bad" (2 Cor. 5:10).

Chapter Seven

THE BIG FIVE

IMAGINE FOR A MOMENT THAT I ask you to go with me on a bike ride. We put on our helmets and I tell you, "Make sure you strap on elbow pads and gloves" because I know something you don't: the spokes are uneven. Sure, we've got great tires and I can even tote you in my basket. But with uneven spokes, I know the tires are going to wobble and collapse and then we are going to crash and fall.

Trying to ride a bike with uneven spokes is like living an out-of-balance life. In this illustration the Big Five (spiritual life, relationships, physical health, finances, and career) are the spokes of your life and the wheel is your calling. You need all of the spokes performing well, the same approximate length, and in tip-top shape to fulfill your calling to glorify God. If they're not, you're going to crash and fall, or at least wobble down the path of life, being ineffective in the kingdom.

TAKING A CLOSER LOOK AT THE BIG FIVE

In the first half of the book, we identified the two main reasons you have been created: to know Christ and to glorify Him. We took a closer look at your passions and gifts and how you can specifically glorify God using both through your calling. We discovered that what you do for Christ on the earth will matter in heaven, and we talked about how to build belief so you can fulfill your calling. All of these are important components for your Blueprint for Life.

In this chapter, I want to show you why it's important to keep the Big Five in balance to support your calling. Then, in each of the upcoming chapters, I will help you create a strategy for each of the Big Five so you can glorify God and make an eternal impact!

To recap from chapter 1, I will help you:

- Develop a *spiritual plan* for maximum intimacy with Christ
- Learn how to leverage and manage your *finances and earthly assets* to make a difference now and for eternity
- Choose and develop a *career path* to support—rather than take away from—your calling
- Develop an intentional plan to nurture and support your most important *relationships*
- Maximize your *physical health* to give you the stamina you need to fulfill your calling

Now, before we move on, let's take a look at six reasons our lives get out of balance.

Desires Run Amok

Experiencing an unbalanced life can happen to the best of us. When this occurs, sometimes it's due to an uncontrollable event such as a tragic accident that causes a strain on our finances, or perhaps a family member becomes terminally ill and we are required to care for them full time. Other times, our lives get out of balance because a desire has run amok. It has become an idol and we think through the fulfillment of it we can get something from it that we can't get from God. When a desire becomes an idol—even if it's intrinsically a good desire such as love or success—we will do anything to serve it, which will lead to an out-of-balance life.

Bill was a driven businessman who traveled nonstop for his job. He often boarded a flight in the morning to fly to Los Angeles or Chicago or some other big city to have business meetings with other high-powered executives. The same day, he would board another flight in the afternoon and arrive in another city for dinner and more meetings. He told himself he would make a lot of money, *then* he would serve God in full-time ministry like he knew God was calling him to—until something happened.

When his five-year-old daughter's teacher asked her, "What does your daddy do?" and she responded, "I don't know but he works at the airport," Bill knew it was time to make a change. His life was out of balance, not to mention he was being disobedient to Christ. And, he was sacrificing his most important relationships for his career all because he valued what he could accomplish and the money he could earn more than he valued doing God's will. When he finally surrendered to God, he experienced peace and a new calling that transformed his life. Then, he was truly glorifying God because he was living the life the Architect intended.

Timothy Keller wrote about how far the tragedy of living an unbalanced life can take us in his book *Counterfeit Gods*:

> After the global economic crisis began in mid-2008, there followed a tragic string of suicides of formerly wealthy and well-connected individuals. The acting chief financial officer of Freddie Mac, the Federal Home Loan Mortgage Corporation, hanged himself in his basement. The chief executive of Sheldon Good, a leading U.S. real estate auction firm, shot himself in the head behind the wheel of his red Jaguar. A French money manager who invested

the wealth of many of Europe's royal and leading families, and who had lost $1.4 billion of his clients' money in Bernard Madoff's Ponzi scheme, slit his wrists and died in his Madison Avenue office. A Danish senior executive with HSBC Bank hanged himself in the wardrobe of his *L500*-a-night suite in Knightsbridge, London.[1]

Sadly when tragedy hit, these men were faced with the reality that they had built their lives on what De Tocqueville called "an incomplete joy of this world"[2] and as a result, their lives were out of balance. Don't get me wrong, there is nothing wrong with money. God has blessed me with money so I can be a blessing to others. But, there is something wrong when you place your hope in it at the expense of following Christ.

Voices everywhere encourage us to value other things more than we value God's will and living for Him. These voices tell us if we have a bigger house, we'll be happy. So we take on a larger mortgage and don't manage our finances well. We don't consider how the strain of a bigger payment means we will have to work longer hours to pay for our debt, which means we'll have less time for our most important relationships. Next thing you know, our relationships have crashed and burned because our lives are out of balance. And because we are so busy picking up our relational pieces, we don't have time to fulfill our calling.

Sometimes the voices tell us if we have a higher-profile career that we'll be satisfied. So we take on a new job we have been dreaming about. The only problem is that it means we won't be able to attend church anymore. So, our relationship with God suffers and our relationships with those we fellowship with suffer too. The next thing you know, we have crashed and burned in our spiritual life, which affects every other area of our life, including our calling.

Or, maybe we go years without taking care of our physical health. We live on junk food, don't exercise, and keep smoking. The next thing you know, we have crashed and burned in our health, which affects our finances because we are spending more and more money on medical bills, which creates a strain in our marriage, which all means we are hindered from living out our calling.

It's clear that an unbalanced life is a chaotic life. This is why it's so important to steward our lives well. One bad "spoke" on the "bike of life" affects all the others and our ability to complete our God-given calling.

To begin to live a balanced life, ask God to reveal to you if your desires are in line with His will. Is there any idolatry in your life that would cause you to live outside the boundaries He has created for you? If none of your desires are out of His will, if nothing has become an idol, if there isn't anything you desire more than doing His will and fulfilling His calling for your life, you are well on your way to living a life of balance.

Keep in mind, there will be seasons now and then when something in life gets out of balance due to some unforeseen event you can't control, such as the death of a family member or job loss. Or, there will be times due to extra added life responsibilities that you have to live out of balance. This happened to me in 2013 with the launch of my new business, iDisciple. During these times, we need to get our lives back in balance as soon as possible. Then, we can continue to glorify God as best as possible.

FEAR

Fear is closely related to idolatry. Sometimes when we are highly fearful, it will cause us to idolize or desire something more than is healthy. For example, if we are highly afraid of failure, we may idolize success. This can cause us to be driven to succeed in such a way that is not God honoring and causes our lives to get out of balance.

Or perhaps we are afraid of rejection so we desire love more than is healthy. For this reason, our relationships get out of balance, which ultimately hinders our calling.

I recently read a post by Julia, a woman on Facebook, who was driven by the fear of failure. This resulted in an unhealthy drive to succeed, which negatively affected her spiritual life. Julia wrote:

> A few years ago, I became extremely driven to succeed. God had placed a dream in my heart for a particular calling, and I was working hard to achieve that dream. What I didn't know is that the fear of failure was driving me to succeed. As a result, I sacrificed intimacy with Christ.
>
> I also no longer found satisfaction in the little blessings He was giving me every day. I became greatly dissatisfied things weren't happening how I wanted and when I wanted. I spent many days wrestling with anger.
>
> When I look back on this season, I see how my expectations and fear of failure robbed me of joy. I thought my desires were good—and at the core, were. I just wanted to serve Christ. But they were misdirected.
>
> One morning, after a long season of wrestling and striving, I awoke and I was at rest. I knew I had finally given in. I was ready

to stop trying to control my life. I would let God have His way instead. "Ah, yes Lord. Now it's just you and me again."

The idol of valuing what I could achieve more than loving Jesus was gone. I sighed in relief. I had come home. He had restored me to a place of loving Him most like I had earlier in my walk with Christ. Oh! How I had missed Him.

What Julia experienced is what can happen to any of us when our lives get out of balance. If we make any area more important than the others, something is going to have to give. If we want to be all we can be for God, then we have to take care of business, not just in our callings, but in the Big Five so that we can glorify Christ.

A Lack of Education

Sometimes our desires aren't out of control because we are idolizing money, status, or material goods. And fear isn't controlling us. Sometimes we are just uninformed about how to manage one or more of the Big Five. Therefore, our lives are out of balance. Maybe we make a bad business investment, or we fail to nurture our marriage the way we should only because we don't know how.

There are times when all of us are uninformed in some life area because all of us are learning how to walk with God and do life His way day by day. Keep in mind there are lots of resources out there—including this book—that can help you begin to live a balanced life to support your calling. (You can also check out my organization iDisciple.org for help with all life areas.) If you know you could do better to keep one of the Big Five of your life aligned so you can live out your calling, begin with this book, then learn all you can to become an expert in the area where you need help.

A Lack of Discipline

Imagine that you love to speed. On side roads, main roads, and highways, you put the pedal to the metal and zip, zoom, and race here and there and everywhere. You just love the thrill of speed. You have gotten some traffic tickets, but you just don't have the discipline to stop driving fast.

The tickets don't affect your life too much until you get more than a few and the fees start piling up. Next thing you know, you lose your license, which causes you to lose your job because you don't have any transportation to get to work—all because you lacked the discipline to stop speeding. Sometimes things out of our control happen that cause our lives to get out of balance. Other times we lack the self-discipline to make necessary changes in our relationships, finances, spiritual lives, career, or physical life. This can also cause an imbalance.

If this describes you, seek out help to make positive changes so you don't experience a negative domino effect that can be a part of an out-of-balance life.

Going Too Fast

In an entertaining message titled "How to Live a Balanced and Blessed Life," Dr. Charles Lowery talks about how we live in a stressful, fast world.

Think about it. If you want to do your finances, it's Quick Books; if you want to call somebody, it's Sprint; if you want to send something, it's Federal Express; if you want to eat something, it's fast food; if you want to diet, it's Slimfast; if you want to eat at home, it's Minute Rice; if you want to drink hot chocolate, it's Nestle's Quick; if you want to get your pictures developed, it's Fast Photo; if you want to get your clothes cleaned, it's One-Hour Cleaners; if you want to get your car fixed, it's 10-Minute Lube; if you want to get to the airport, it's rapid shuttle; if you want to get to the hotel, it's express check-in. Even when you want to relax, and get out your swim suit, what do they call it? It's called Speedo. It's a fast world, isn't it?[3]

This fast-paced world can make us think we can do more and more and more until one day we wake up and realize that we can't do any more, we are fed up, and our lives are out of balance. A wise person knows their limitations; they know how much they can accomplish, and in what time frame they can accomplish it. They are mindful that the world may be moving fast, but that doesn't mean they have to keep up. They implement rest into their life so they can go the distance with God in their calling, to avoid an unbalanced life, and avoid burnout.

Like a long-distance runner, they pace themselves. They know how to plan within their God-given boundaries. They recognize their limitations and know they can't do everything, but they can focus on the Big Five and their calling. They can do a few things well, but perfection is not possible. When they recognize their limitations, they work as a co-laborer with Christ but leave the results of their calling to Christ, as a demonstration of their trust in Him.

Keepin' Up with the Joneses

A pastor once gave a sermon during which he said, "Everyone's plate is a different size." This is an interesting thought that highlights a truth that we have all been created differently to take on different tasks and different task loads. When we understand this, it will help us live balanced lives because we will stop thinking we have to live the life of our neighbor. There won't be any keeping up with the Joneses!

Because everyone's plate is a different size, God hasn't put on my plate what He has put on yours. So, you may be able to carry a load I can't. Or, I may be able to master a particular calling you are unable to, because it's not how you have been created.

Because my plate is a particular size, it means I have been uniquely designed to carry out a particular calling and manage my Big Five in particular ways. Therefore, I do not beat myself up that I am not doing what you are doing. I know I uniquely fill a particular role in God's kingdom.

How wonderful that we can all be exactly who God has created us to be! It's awesome I can live a balanced life that has been custom designed by the Creator for me. I never have to fret and try to live out someone else's calling.

The minute I agree that God has, in His sovereignty, placed on my plate what He hasn't placed on yours, is the minute I can celebrate your accomplishments—and I can be content with mine. The word *comparison* is no longer in my vocabulary and so I am not driven to be something I am not. I do not criticize you for doing too much or not enough. And I am not jealous or wishing I could do what you are doing. Instead, I rejoice in what you accomplish. And, I am equally grateful for what God is doing through me for His glory (2 Thess. 1:12).

I see myself in the context of a greater whole with each one of God's children uniquely serving Him with their gifts and talents.

When I realize that what is on my plate has been placed there by my Creator, I also know He will empower me to do what He has called me to (Phil. 4:13). For this reason, I can always be successful in my calling. I must remember He will not empower me to do what someone else is doing if that is not my assignment. And, if I try to take on someone else's calling, I may experience an out-of-balance, stressful life because God has not equipped me to complete a calling He has not designed for me. Everyone's plate is a different size.

True Success Includes Balance

Just as an eternal perspective is important to avoid living a wasted life, so is balance. Without balance you won't be able to go the distance and create a life that is pleasing to God. As you develop your Blueprint for Life, it needs to take into account your spiritual life, relationships, physical well-being, finances, and career. Success in one or two areas isn't success to God. He designed us to be well rounded.

There's nothing wrong with providing well for your family or making sacrifices to be successful. But when you sacrifice the very thing God cares about in those efforts, you'll miss the life God intended for you. If the demands of your career leave little or zero time for your spiritual growth, is it worthwhile? If you achieve all your financial goals but ruin your health as a result, have you benefitted? Even if your calling impacts God's kingdom but your children feel neglected, is it worth it? You can only live the life of impact you were designed for when you're following God's blueprint for every area of life.

In the upcoming chapters, we'll take a closer look at the Big Five and develop a strategy for each one to keep your life in balance and support your calling.

Eternal Perspective Scripture

"Therefore, my dear friends, as you have always obeyed—not only in my presence, but now much more in my absence—continue to work out your salvation with fear and trembling, for it is God who works in you to will and to act in order to fulfill his good purpose" (Phil. 2:12–13 UPDATED NIV).

Chapter Eight

YOUR SPIRITUAL
STRATEGY

I N 1960 PAUL CARRACK SANG a song called "I Need You." In it, he sings how he needs the one he loves like a ball needs a game, and like a pool needs a cue.

Without a game a ball has no purpose; without a cue a pool game isn't going to happen. There are some things that just go together. One needs the other. Your calling is the same; it can't exist without God. It begins and ends in Him.

Your relationship with Christ is also important because it's the foundation for your entire life. Your relationship with God affects your career, finances, relationships, and physical life. The decisions you make in these areas are a direct result of your relationship with Him. This is why you need an intentional strategy to develop your spiritual life.

Developing this strategy isn't a way to earn favor with God so you can get what you want. It's not about being "good enough" or religious. It's about responding to His invitation for you to know Him intimately, live for Him, and demonstrate your love for Him. (Remember this is one of the main reasons you are here.) This will lead to the abundant, eternal life you seek and that He promises to those who know Him (John 3:16–18). This is the only way you can be truly successful in your calling.

There are many ideas out there about how to get to know Christ better, including implementing spiritual disciplines into one's daily life, such as solitude, confession, and fasting. In this chapter, I want to investigate three top disciplines that will help you grow in your relationship with Christ: Bible study, prayer, and fellowship.

BIBLE STUDY

In his video "Coffee with God," Pastor Bill Hybels tells an engaging story of a new Christian who was a hard-charging advertising executive. The man told Bill he didn't have time to meet with God and read his Bible because of his daily responsibilities and work commute. Bill responded, "I have always been able to make time for stuff I value. I'm making time for a meeting with God in my life. You can do it however you want." The man wasn't too happy with Bill's response and walked away.

Several months later Bill saw the man again. His countenance had changed, and he invited Bill and his wife to dinner. A short time after the Hybels arrived at the man's home, the man ushered Bill to a rocking chair.

"I have a little backyard here and I love looking out . . . So I bought this chair to look out over the yard. Each morning I get up fifteen to thirty minutes early. I sit in the chair. I have a cup of coffee. I read God's Word. I try to make sense of it. I ask Him to speak to me by His Word. Then I meditate on it, reflect on it, and apply it to my life. Then I write some thoughts down in a journal and I pray that I will be more aware of His presence."

"How's that going for you?" Bill asked.

His wife jumped in and said, "I'll tell you how it's going. He's a changed guy. What happens to him when he sits in that chair has changed him. He's more centered. He's more gentle, and more loving in our marriage."

Many months later the man told Bill that he was thinking of leaving his job in advertising. "I think I am done with that," he said.

"Where did you get these ideas?" Bill asked.

"In my meetings with God in the chair. He's been putting those thoughts in my mind."

Then the man offered to volunteer at Willow Creek Community Church where Bill pastors while using some of his money from his advertising career to support his family. He was a blessing at Willow Creek and served at the church for many years as a dedicated worker.

Years passed and the man told Bill he had gotten another idea while sitting in his chair. He felt God was calling him to relocate to Colorado to serve at a new startup church. So he returned to the marketplace and donated much of the money he earned to his new church.

Years later, the man became ill with cancer and was admitted to the hospital. He was saddened that he didn't have his chair with him.

After he passed away, the man's wife told Bill, "His whole life changed in that chair. We are going to pass it on to our children and our grandchildren in the hopes that someone's life will be transformed like his."[1]

This man's life was transformed because he experienced intimacy with Christ through prayer and His Word. In the chair, his love grew for God, as well as others—and He received direction for his life and calling. God wants to do the same for you.

Like this man was at first, so many people are so busy doing good, being productive, living their lives, and maybe even doing good for God they don't make time to be still before their Maker. But if we want to live the abundant life Christ promised (John 10:10), if we want to fulfill the two main reasons we are here—to know Christ and to glorify God—if we want to make a difference while we have our breath, we must spend time with Him. Your calling begins and ends in Him. He is the Source of your calling—and apart from Him you can do nothing (John 15:5). Don't make the tragic mistake of spending your entire life neglecting your time with Him, only to later realize what treasured time you missed with your Creator and that you could have had a fuller, more productive life for Christ if you had known Him better. Don't make the mistake of attempting to pursue your calling apart from Christ.

Do you have a chair? Do you have a place where you can commune regularly with Christ and become aware of His presence in your life? Hybels says your "chair" can be anywhere. It can be in your bedroom closet, your car, or a corner booth at your favorite coffee shop. The important thing is to spend time with Christ. Intentionally carve out a specific time each day to hear from Him and share your life with Him. The marvelous thing is that you will discover that the more time you spend with Him, the more time you will want to spend with Him.

My "chair" is in my study. And, if I have a lot to do in the morning, my place is in my car, where I listen to God's Word through my smartphone on an audio Bible app. Each morning I connect with Christ to learn from Him and hear what He has to say. It is an important spiritual discipline that has given me the needed wisdom to navigate the business world and face many of the challenges that are a part of launching new ventures.

Making a Plan

If you don't already spend regular quiet time with God, the thought may feel intimidating. Some people believe they have to spend hours and hours in prayer and Bible study. Keep in mind that just like the man in Bill's story, you can begin with just fifteen minutes of undistracted time. You might choose to read a devotional, or you may want to study your way through the Bible verse by verse. There isn't one right way to do it. Choose a plan that is comfortable for you. If you aren't sure where to start, there are many Bible study methods and helps online.

Here is one simple method from author and Bible teacher Anne Graham Lotz:

1. Read God's Word (It may be a chapter, or something shorter, such as just a few verses)
2. List the facts (What does God's Word say?)
3. Learn the lessons (What does God's Word mean?)
4. Listen to His voice (What does God's Word mean to *me*?)[2]

Write down your answers to each of the above in a journal. You'll be amazed at how consistent time in God's Word will transform your life and give you guidance to support your calling so you can glorify Him well and make an eternal impact!

PRAYER

Some people define prayer as only petition. Others say it's expressing gratitude to God, only praying for others, or seeking guidance. Some believe we can pray to God through tears, shouts, or whispers; bow our heads; or pray with our eyes wide open. The truth is that prayer is all of these things.

You can toss short popcorn prayers up to heaven as you shower, brush your teeth, drive to work, and eat your lunch. You can flood God's throne room all day long with conversation in the form of petitions, praise, adoration, and confession. And, you can spend longer times communing with Him in silence and solitude. The important thing is to talk with Him, share your heart, and listen for His voice.

Five-year-old Samantha often had nightmares during which she would scream and wake up her family. One late night her father came into her room and asked, "What are you afraid of?"

"The monsters," she said.

Her father replied, "Would you like to pray and ask the monsters to go away?"

Samantha nodded, held her father's hands, and prayed a short one-sentence prayer: "Jesus, please make the monsters go away."

When Samantha was grown, her father told her that her nightmares had stopped that night.

Of course, not all problems are solved as easily, but my point is that prayer doesn't have to be complicated, sound religious, or follow a formula, because prayer is just talking to God in sincerity of heart.

In her study *Living So That*, Wendy Blight wrote:

I grew up reciting rote prayers with my eyes closed and my head bowed. Jesus broke the mold for me. He was a man of prayer who prayed continually. He prayed in so many places and in many ways. His prayers never looked the same. Sometimes He withdrew and prayed alone. Sometimes He prayed in the presence of others. Sometimes He prayed prayers of praise. Sometimes He prayed prayers of desperation. Sometimes He prayed for others. Sometimes He prayed for Himself. Sometimes He prayed early in the morning. Sometimes He prayed in the middle of the day.

Jesus' example teaches us that we can pray whenever and wherever we feel called to pray. There are no rules. We can pray silently or out loud. We can pray alone or together. We can pray driving a car or lying on our beds. We can pray with our heads bowed and eyes closed or heads lifted and eyes wide open.[3]

What a magnificent thing that the Creator of the universe invites us to talk with Him! God wants to know you and for you to know Him through prayer!

Here are a few other facts about prayer that I think you will find interesting as they relate to your calling:

Prayer will make you more spiritually sensitive.

When you spend focused time in prayer, there will be times when the Lord will show you what He plans to do in your life or in your calling. He may reveal His plans to you through a picture He brings to mind, an internal knowing, or the "still, small voice" of the Holy Spirit. In short, prayer will create an environment for God to align your heart with His. Prayer will give you spiritual antennae so you begin to notice in your circumstances what He has revealed to you. Prayer will make you more spiritually sensitive to His will.

In his book *Draw the Circle*, Mark Batterson wrote: "Prayer is the difference between seeing with our physical eyes and seeing with our spiritual eyes. Prayer gives us God's-eye view. It heightens awareness and gives us a sixth sense that enables us to perceive spiritual realities that are beyond our five senses."[4]

In their classic book *Geeks & Geezers*,[5] business gurus Warren Bennis and Robert Thomas make an interesting observation about a common denominator among successful leaders in every field. Bennis and Thomas call them "first class noticers." Being a first-class noticer allows you to recognize talent, identify opportunities, and avoid pitfalls. Leaders who succeed again and again are geniuses at grasping context. This is one of those characteristics, like taste, that is difficult to break down into its component parts. But the ability to weigh a welter of factors, some as subtle as how different groups of people will interpret a gesture, is one of the hallmarks of a great leader.

Prayer turns us into first-class noticers. It helps us see what God wants us to notice. The more you pray, the more you notice; the less you pray, the less you notice. It's as simple as that.

Prayer is an open line of communication to God to hear His heart and discover His will. Don't get so busy that you forget to talk to Him. In addition to making you more spiritually sensitive, prayer will give you guidance.

Bring on the guidance.

Before Dr. Elmer Towns was the co-founder of Liberty University, the largest Christian university in the United States, he was offered an opportunity to work for the National Sunday School Association, traveling, speaking, and teaching to various denominations on their behalf. It seemed like the perfect opportunity for national recognition, influence, and a wider ministry, much more so than he had at the teaching job he currently held at a small Bible college. But then he had an encounter with God in prayer that changed his direction.

Towns wrote about the experience in his book *God Encounters*:

> I woke up violently in the middle of the black night. Something was wrong. I began to sweat all over.
>
> "Lord, what is it?"
>
> The Lord was in the room, not physically, nor did I see a

vision, nor did I hear an audible voice; but I knew that the Lord was standing by my bed to warn me of something . . . I prayed several times, "Lord, what are you trying to tell me?"

Then the Lord spoke to my heart, telling me not to take the new job I had just accepted . . . "Don't take the job," God kept saying.[6]

Taking the job seemed like the right thing to do considering his gifts and talents, and how he could make the greatest impact. Not only that, but ever since Towns was a freshman in college he had wanted to be a Bible college president. This opportunity looked like a fast track to his dream.

However, after wrestling with God for a couple of hours in prayer, Towns realized he was being driven by his ego. So he told the Lord that fame was not important and that he wouldn't take the job—even if it meant never becoming a college president.

Then the Lord spoke to his heart, *Don't take the Sunday school job . . . but within a year I will give you a college presidency.* He obeyed, continued to teach at the small Bible college, and kept trusting God.

One wintry day two months later, he decided to stop by his church to chat with his pastor, Robert MacMillan. While there, he told Pastor MacMillan about his dream to become a Bible college president. "That's wonderful!" the pastor responded, then told Towns he had the talent to do the job. Just then the phone rang. It was a pastor friend of MacMillan's from Toronto, Canada, who asked, "Do you know where I can find a young man to be president of Winnipeg Bible College?"

"Your man is sitting right here," MacMillan answered.

Because Dr. Towns was open to hearing from God in prayer, he received God's guidance and direction about his future calling.

Remember to keep a clear channel of communication open between you and Christ and *expect* Him to reveal truth to you during various seasons.

I hope you have been encouraged to just start talking to God all the time, every day, in all kinds of circumstances. Prayer will prove to be a dynamic way He guides you.

Here are some additional helpful tips for developing a strong prayer life to support your life and calling.

1. RECORD YOUR PRAYERS. Some people like to keep a prayer journal to record their conversations with God. This can be especially powerful when they revisit their entries and see what God has done. I have heard of others who keep a prayer poster on the wall. On this poster, they record the prayer, the date of the prayer, and the answers for petition. So often, we pray and then forget what we prayed about. A prayer poster provides a visual reminder of God's faithfulness, answers, and guidance.

2. PRAY ALL KINDS OF PRAYERS AND REQUESTS. In Scripture, Paul says to pray all kinds of prayers and requests (Eph. 6:18). As I mentioned, there are no rules for prayer and you can pray in various ways and times. Prayer is much more than petition. Prayer includes praising Him, confessing sin, thanking Him for what He has done and is going to do still, and worshipping Him.

3. PRAY IN SUBMISSION. I wonder if God ever feels like His people approach Him more like a divine vending machine than as a loving Father. Remember, our lives are not our own. In all things when you pray, remember we are to submit to Christ. Jesus said He came to do the will of His Father (John

6:38). Our prayer lives are to be a reflection of the submission of our hearts just as Jesus' prayer life was a reflection of His.

4. PRAY DARING PRAYERS. Some people spend their lives praying safe prayers and only what they know they can accomplish in their own strength—and what they accomplish in their calling is a reflection of the lack of depth of their belief of what God can do. God wants you to pray daring, believing prayers in all areas of life and for your calling. What you can do in your own strength is only the beginning of how God can use you for Him. Can you imagine what would happen if you dared to pray for that which you thought was impossible?

FELLOWSHIP WITH OTHER BELIEVERS

When we experience fellowship with others in the context of a community of believers, whether it's in a home church, a megachurch, or a small group, we understand in a greater way what it means to be connected to our own hearts and to the heart of God. Others mirror God's heart to us; they teach us truths about love, and forgiveness, and how to live a Christian life the way the Architect intended. As we watch others walk out their faith, we discover what it means to be fully alive in the body of Christ, using our gifts and passions for Him. But when we isolate ourselves and wander away from others who know the Savior, we miss out on experiencing Christ on so many levels. God designed us to connect with others. It's a vital part of your spiritual strategy.

In a story called "The Lonely Ember," Dr. John MacArthur tells about a man who had regularly attended church, but then stopped going. On a brisk evening, the pastor decided to visit the man. He found him sitting in front of a fire.

After the pastor situated himself in a chair near the flames, he considered the burning logs. Without saying a word, the pastor carefully took some tongs, chose a burning ember, and gently placed it on the hearth. Then he sat back down and watched.

The ember glowed momentarily, but then its fire was no more.

Neither of the men had spoken a word during their meeting. But just before the pastor left, he picked up the dead ember and placed it back in the fire. It glowed as the other embers burned around it.

As the pastor reached the door, the man said, "Thank you so much for your visit and especially for the fiery sermon. I shall be back in church next Sunday."[7]

Dr. MacArthur's story is a powerful reminder that it's important to stay plugged into a Christian community as part of your spiritual strategy. Community feeds the "Christ fire" inside us. MacArthur's story also illustrates that our relationship with Christ is not just about us. When we are on fire for Christ and love God, others will catch our passion and be ignited as well. You also don't know how your faith, burning brightly, will positively affect someone you will never meet, maybe a friend of a friend—or even someone in your future family.

In his book *God's Blogs*, Lanny Donoho wrote, "A thread makes its way through history and you are tied to it."[8] Lanny's statement clearly illustrates that your connection with Christ isn't just about burning brightly for your own joy here and now. It's also about others who can only come to Jesus because they see the gospel being preached through your life.

I came to know Christ because someone who was on fire for God shared his faith with me. Who was on fire for Jesus so that you came to know Him too?

Give someone else the gift of joy, love, and salvation you have freely received by keeping your faith burning brightly. It's part of your spiritual strategy.

In closing, here are two more thoughts about growing close to Christ through an intentional plan.

LOVE WILL COMPEL YOU

As you share more and more of your life with Christ and grow through an intentional spiritual strategy, your love for Him will grow and compel you to do good works and to live out your calling.

In 2 Corinthians 5:13–14 Paul told the Corinthians how compelling loving Christ can be. "For if we are beside ourselves, it is for God; or if we are of sound mind, it is for you. For the love of Christ compels us, because we judge thus: that if One died for all, then all died."

In *Condensed Chicken Soup for the Soul,* Dan Millman shares a story about a little girl named Liza who was suffering from a rare and serious disease. The only way that she could recover would be if her five-year-old brother, who had survived the same disease and had developed the antibodies to fight the disease, would give his blood for a transfusion. The doctor told the little boy what Liza needed and then asked if he would give his blood to his sister. He hesitated for a second, took a deep breath, and said, "Yes. I'll do it if it will save Liza."

As the little boy lay next to his sister during the transfusion, the color started returning to her cheeks, but his face grew pale and his smiled faded. Then he looked up at the doctor and asked, "Will I start to die right away?"[9]

Oh! The power of love! He thought he was going to have to give her *all* his blood.

119

The more you partner with God and experience Him through your spiritual strategy, the more your faith and love for Him will compel you, move you, and push you forward to live out your calling for Him and do what you would have thought was impossible.

GOD WANTS YOU TO FIND HIM

Let me encourage you . . . You can have a vibrant, growing, intimate relationship with God. You can know Him so well that you consider Him your best friend.

Do you remember playing hide-and-seek growing up? Did you wait in a hall closet while your heart pounded, hoping like mad that no one would find you?

God doesn't hide where He can't be found, but invites us to look for Him and find Him when He says, "You will seek me and find me when you seek me with all your heart" (Jer. 29:13 NIV).

In Hebrew, the word *seek* specifically involves seeking God through prayer and worship. I love this because God isn't found by following a long list of legalistic rules and religious regulations. Instead, He's found as we seek Him in sincerity of heart.

If we doubt He is listening, this scripture provides encouragement that He hears us. He guarantees that when you seek Him with all your heart, you will find Him. There's no wondering if you'll find Him, no doubting if you'll be able to make your way to Him, or no chance that you won't be allowed to find Him. He will show Himself to you when you genuinely search for Him.

Remember, you can search for Him through many ways, including Bible study, prayer, and fellowship. The goal is not to be a perfect Christian. God is more concerned with the condition of your heart, that you desire to seek Him, not that you seek Him perfectly. I hope this encourages you today to begin to develop your spiritual strategy.

ETERNAL PERSPECTIVE SCRIPTURE

"But you, when you pray, go into your room, and when you have shut your door, pray to your Father who is in the secret place; and your Father who sees in secret will reward you openly" (Matt. 6:6).

Chapter Nine

YOUR RELATIONAL STRATEGY

I F YOU WENT TO COLLEGE prior to 1985, you probably remember those late nights romancing a typewriter and a cup of coffee while you pounded out a term paper. What I remember about those papers isn't just that I sometimes added to my stress level by waiting until the last minute to write them, but I had to do a lot of research and add those sources of my research in the form of footnotes.

First Corinthians 13 reminds us that love is not a footnote in God's book. It's not something extra to be added after we have fulfilled our calling, or identified our passions and gifts. Instead, love is the framework that our passions, gifts, calling, and finances, as well as every other area of our lives, should center around. The apostle Paul wrote,

> Though I speak with the tongues of men and of angels, but have not love, I have become sounding brass or a clanging cymbal. And though I have the gift of prophecy, and understand all mysteries and all knowledge, and though I have all faith, so that I could remove mountains, but have not love, I am nothing. And though I bestow all my goods to feed the poor, and though I give my body to be burned, but have not love, it profits me nothing. . . . And now abide faith, hope, love, these three; but the greatest of these is love. (vv. 1–3, 13)

In a podcast by John Eldredge titled "Loving God Means Loving Others," John said:

We think the greatest impact for the kingdom has to do with either size, like "Wow! We have a huge church." Or "Wow! We have a massive missions effort" or "Wow! We're selling lots of books" or "Wow! Sixty thousand people came to this conference."

Or we think [the proof of making an impact for the kingdom] is some incredible level of gifting. "Wow! She is just an amazing teacher" or "She's such a talented counselor." Or, "Wow! He's so prophetic. He sees into the mysterious things of God." And, here's the mind-blowing thing . . . God doesn't think so. Again, 1 Corinthians 13 is [saying], "You can have all that stuff, but love is actually greater than all of it."[1]

It's possible to be the picture of health, invest monetarily in God's work, have a great career using your passions and gifts, and still be unsuccessful in God's eyes if we don't love those around us well. Don't misunderstand me, I don't believe making a big impact through a large organization or a large church or a massive missions effort is bad. In fact, I am a huge advocate of pulling the biggest levers you can in your life to glorify God and make an impact on eternity. However, without love, anything we do has no value to God (1 Cor. 13:2).

This is why it's important for your Blueprint for Life to include what I call a "relational strategy." This relational strategy will help you love well. It's an *intentional plan* to help you prioritize, manage, nurture, and support your most valuable relationships. And like the other Big Five, this plan should support—not take away from—your calling.

A solid relational strategy will help you decide . . .

- *Who* you need to invest time in
- *When* you need to spend that time
- *How* you need to spend it

DEFINE YOUR CIRCLES

Every person alive has a "relational portfolio" that consists of people such as their spouse, children, family members, friends, and co-workers. For Christians, this portfolio often includes other relationships as well that play an important role to help you achieve goals related to God's calling for your life. You may have relationships with a pastor, a mentor, accountability partners, or fellowship groups. It's important to remember that every relationship either supports or does not support your calling and Blueprint for Life.

To develop a solid relational strategy, first you need to identify which relationships are most important in your relationship portfolio. You can easily do this by thinking of your relationships as a series of circles.

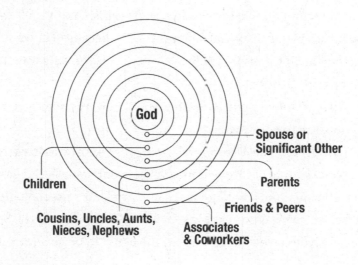

Circle #1: God in the Center

Maybe like me when you were a kid, you drew on the sidewalk. Imagine standing on a sidewalk with a piece of your favorite colored chalk in hand. Now imagine drawing a circle around yourself. This is what I call your inner circle, and it represents the most important relationship in your relationship portfolio; it's your relationship with God.

In Matthew 22:37 Jesus described how important our relationship with Him should be when He said, "Love the Lord your God with all your heart and with all your soul and with all your mind" (NIV).

Without an intimate and growing relationship with God, all of your relationships will suffer—and your calling will too.

Circle #2: Your Mate

Next, imagine drawing a slightly bigger circle outside the first one. Now, write your mate's name inside. If you are not married, the next closest relationship may be a close friend or a significant other.

God designed the marital relationship to be the most important after your relationship with God. He doesn't ask you to put your spouse second after Him because He is selfish and wants to make you miserable or deny your happiness. It's because He wants to be glorified in all things in our lives. And, this is the only way that you will be truly fulfilled.

Also, when you put Him first, you'll have more to give in your relationship to your mate.

In his book *The Meaning of Marriage,* Timothy Keller wrote, "If your only source of love and meaning is your spouse, then anytime he or she fails you, it will not just cause grief but a psychological cataclysm. If, however, you know something of the work of the Spirit in your life, you have enough love 'in the bank' to be generous to your spouse even when you are not getting much affection or kindness at the moment."[2]

In addition to placing Christ first so that you have enough "love in the bank," there are ways that you can make deposits in your relationship through your relational strategy. We'll talk about more specifics in the upcoming pages.

Circle #3: Your Children

Now imagine drawing a third circle outside and around the first two. This circle represents your relationship with your kids. The Bible calls children a blessing and inheritance from the Lord (Ps. 127:3). Your relationship with them should reflect this perspective.

Children are very important, but some people make the mistake of prioritizing their kids over their mate. Because child raising is demanding, it can be easy for this to happen. So you must be deliberate in keeping your kids third. One of the best gifts you can give to your kids is to show them what a successful marriage looks like. This will give them a sense of stability as they experience life challenges.

Since your child's communication skills are still developing, he is not likely to tell you when he requires love and attention. In fact, he probably doesn't even understand his own feelings and needs. So it's up to you to be intentional in your relationship so neither you nor your child end up regretting the time you didn't spend together.

In 1974, Harry Chapin wrote "Cat's in the Cradle," a song about a busy working man who passes up years of opportunities to spend time with his son. In the end, the tune takes a turn when the son grows up and is too busy to spend time with his father. Unfortunately, this man lives with the regret of not loving his son well.

This song is a sobering reminder that minutes quickly turn

129

into days and days into months that turn into years. Because time passes so fast, and because the tyranny of the urgent can override what is truly important, it's critical that your relationship with your kids is a priority and that you have a relational strategy. Otherwise you'll end up wishing you had made your most important relationships, most important.

Circle #4: Your Parents

Next, draw a circle outside the last one. This circle represents the relationship you have with your parents.

Although my parents live nearby, it would be easy to go for a few weeks without ever seeing them because they don't get out much. Therefore, I have a relational strategy to go to their home at least once a week for a cup of coffee. I stay for a few hours just to talk and catch up without distractions.

Additionally, each winter when they spend the colder months in Panama City, Florida, I travel out of town to visit. As my parents age, I know I have a limited number of opportunities to show them how much they mean to me, and I know I will cherish our times together after they have gone home to heaven.

Matthew 7:12 is a good reminder about spending time with parents. How much time will your kids spend with you in your twilight years? Chances are, they are watching how much time you spend with your parents and they will most likely follow in your footsteps. If you want your kids to spend time with you in your later years, spend time with your parents.

Circle #5: Your Extended Family

The next circle you would draw represents your extended family —your cousins, aunts and uncles, nieces and nephews. Although you may not see these people as often as your immediate family, your parents, or even your friends, they are a vital part of your relational strategy. Make a point to get to know these people. That may mean making the effort to spend time with these people through reunions or regular family gatherings.

Circle #6: Friends and Peers

The next circle to draw represents the relationship you have with your friends. Remember that the relationships you have with your friends are a powerful component for your calling. They are the vehicle God uses to promote us, encourage us, mature us, and grow us more into His image. But if we choose to associate with the wrong people, we can forfeit our effectiveness for Christ.

Proverbs 12:26 says, "The righteous should choose his friends carefully, for the way of the wicked leads them astray." Choosing carefully means being cautious, as when crossing the street or making a big purchase. Remember, the relationships you choose are one of the greatest determining factors of your level of success in your calling.

Circle #7: Your Associates and Co-workers

The seventh circle is self-explanatory. It's the folks you spend the most time with every day because you are with them at business meetings, in the office, in the field, or in the kitchen cooking up dinner for your restaurant. When it comes to this group, pray for wisdom and ask God to show you who to be close to and who to invest time in outside the office.

Now that we have identified your circles, let's take a look at how to develop a relational strategy and what to do once you have developed it.

GIVE A QUANTITY OF QUALITY TIME

Every good relational strategy must contain a quantity of quality time. That means you dedicate an amount of time and give someone your undivided attention. According to Dr. Gary Chapman, this kind of quality time is a powerful emotional communicator of love and is a central aspect of togetherness.

Lots of people spend a *quantity* of time with the people in their life, but it's not quality. For example, a couple may spend multiple nights each week sitting on the couch watching television together, but this isn't quality time. They can go to a party together, but never speak with one another, so it's not quality time.

Two people can be married and live in the same house without knowing each other more than they do their acquaintances. Children can spend time with their parents but not feel as if Mom and Dad really want to understand them. Friends can talk to one another, but not feel as though they are being heard. Sharing square footage or spending lots of hours together doesn't mean a good relationship will develop.

Regardless of the type of relationship, if it's with your spouse, children, or friends, you need a plan to not only spend time with them, but make sure that the time you do spend with them is quality—that it makes an impact. Healthy relationships require a quantity of quality time.

Here are a few things you can do to make sure that the time you spend together isn't just quantity, but that it's also quality:

Give the person you are with your full attention.

Just like Dr. Gary Chapman says, quality time involves giving someone your full attention. If you go out to eat with your mate, talk with him or her. Make open-ended statements such as, "Tell me about your day," and ask open-ended questions such as, "What is God teaching you?" Ask what they have been wrestling with, what they are happy about, and how you can serve them better. While they are answering, don't be thinking about the next thing that you want to say. Don't interrupt, and make sure you look them in the eye. If you spend time with your children, practice the same sensitive actions.

It always bothers me when I see couples out to dinner sharing a table, but not sharing themselves because they are both either texting or talking on their cell phones. A good rule in this technology-driven age is not to have your phone during meal times so you can give the one you care for the attention he or she deserves.

Discover their interests and spend time in the right environment.

Imagine I decide that I would like to take you fishing. I am excited about the thought of taking you on an adventure that involves going to the outdoors, sleeping in a tent, and cooking hot dogs on an open grill. But there is one problem: you have told me you don't like camping, that you are allergic to mosquitos, and that you think fishing is boring. While this kind of activity sounds like great quality time to me, it would be the exact opposite for you.

To make sure you spend a quantity of quality time with your loved ones, get involved in their interests and make sure you spend time in the *right environment that meets their needs.* This will enhance your relationship and will be a sacrificial way to practice loving. If your child likes roller skating, take him or her skating. If your husband enjoys taking pictures while on walks along a river and would like your company, go. Just make sure that you spend your time together, that it's quality time, and that you are giving your full attention to the one you are with.

Build in tradition.

Traditions can be another important aspect of quality time. Every important relationship in your life can include traditions that create lasting memories and foster closeness. For example, every week, I have a date night with my wife. This is a tradition we have enjoyed for years that has helped us stay connected in the midst of raising kids, managing a household, and operating my businesses.

One man I know has had the tradition of taking each of his children on a regular date night since they were eighteen months old. On the anniversary of their birth date each month, he takes them to their favorite restaurant. It's something the kids have always looked forward to and has shown them how much they mean to their dad.

Traditions that include a quantity of quality time can be built into all of your relationships—with your mate, children, parents, extended family, and friends . . . even with your co-workers.

Take time away.

Hal White, COO for iDisciple, once attended a conference during which he had the opportunity to talk with the presenter, a pastor of men. Hal asked him, "What is the one thing you have learned about marriage that you could share with me?" The pastor said, "Nothing replaces spending quality time with your spouse." He then told Hal that not only should every couple strive to dialogue daily, and date weekly, but they should also depart quarterly.

There is something about departing—or taking time away— with loved ones that encourages quality time and creates bonds

between people. Taking time away means getting away from your
daily life for a weekend road trip, a longer vacation, or maybe just a
night in a hotel across town.

While the principle of taking time away applies easily to a marriage, it can also apply to your relationships with your kids, friends,
or co-workers. My good friend's wife takes time away with her best
girlfriends twice a year. They rent out a vacation home and do what
they love to do. They go shopping, visit the hair salon, and watch
movies. These deliberate times away strengthen these relationships.

In the mid-1990s I took time away with my family to Disney
World. I knew this would be quality time they would like. We
would be doing something they love in the perfect environment
for kids. But at that time in my life my investment banking company was growing and it was hard to get away from the demands
of work. I regret that I walked through the Magic Kingdom with a
stroller in one hand and my cell phone in the other while talking
on the phone.

Don't forget that if you are not giving your full attention to
those you love when you are with them it doesn't matter where you
are; it won't be quality time.

Put it on your calendar.

I have always said, "If it doesn't show up on your calendar, you
probably won't do it." And, if it doesn't show up on your calendar, it's
probably not a priority or a priority relationship. To spend a quantity of quality time with those in your life, you must make spending
time with them a deliberate priority by *scheduling it.*

In today's world, there are so many distractions in life, and if
you do not protect the relationships that are most important to you,
life will take over and you will end up pushing the things that are

the least urgent to the background, including the management of your relationships.

I have heard that if you want to know where someone's affections lie, take a look at his or her checkbook and calendar. You will spend your money and time on what you value most. It has been said that love is spelled T-I-M-E. And this time will be represented on your calendar.

Now, I'd like to share some specific relational strategies for your mate and children.

YOUR MATE

Some people think there is something unromantic about being strategic in a love relationship. After all, an exciting love relationship should involve emotions and spontaneity! But a long-term, healthy, thriving relationship requires a certain level of planning. Anyone can fall in love, but it takes work to stay that way.

Here are some practical things you can include in your relational strategy with your mate to keep love alive.

Have a regular date night.

In a blog titled, "The Best Thing for Your Kids Is for You to Leave" Ted Lowe, the president and founder of MarriedPeople, an organization dedicated to helping couples enrich their marriages, said, "My wife and I go on a date almost every week. We take a few hours each week just for us. We work out together, see movies, have a meal, we talk, ask each other silly questions, and do that other fun thing couples do. We have uninterrupted time to re-connect. Dating lifts our heads from the chaos of kids and work, and makes us see each other. Dating matters. It really matters, but not just for us, for our kids."[3]

Carol Ummel Lindquist, Ph.D., said, "The irony is that a strong relationship with your spouse is one of the best things you can do for your kids. You and your spouse are modeling a good relationship, which sets your children up for better marriages themselves when they grow up."[4]

Some couples don't have a regular date night because they feel they don't have the time or the money. And, small children can make getting out of the house challenging. Keep in mind that your date night doesn't have to be extravagant, long, expensive, or complicated.

I recently heard about one couple that had several small children. Their oldest son told his parents that they could go out because he would watch the smaller children. He wanted to prove that he was growing up and becoming more responsible, so he told them they didn't need a sitter. The couple was concerned and didn't want to get too far away from home for too long, so they drove their car to a street not too far away, parked in the cul-de-sac, opened the car doors, turned on the radio, and danced in the street. Approximately thirty minutes later, they were back at home, no one had died, the house hadn't burned down, and they had a successful date night.

Avoid a trip to the dog house.

As I said at the beginning of this chapter, when you go out on a date with your mate, make sure you give them your full attention. This will make them feel special. I made the mistake of not following this rule when I once went on a date with my wife—on Valentine's Day.

I can hear you groaning. And you should be. I made a mistake that landed me in the dog house for a long time. As any good husband should do, I invited my wife, Michele, out to a very nice restaurant for a romantic evening. We were seated at our table, the ambience was just right, Michele looked beautiful, and we were in the middle of our meal having a good conversation when I made the mistake of answering my phone. My business partner was calling and, well . . . it could be important! One minute turned into two, then three, then ten, then fifty. I was on the phone with my partner for almost an hour, and with each ticking minute, I could see Michele was becoming more and more irritated. And rightly so! My actions showed her that I didn't value her. I have learned not to break the important relational strategy to give your full attention to the one you are with!

Don't make it a business meeting.

I have always thought the best date nights are those when spouses focus on each other without turning the date into a business meeting. That said, I believe the best relational strategy for any date night is to:

1. Not talk about money
2. Not talk about problems
3. Not talk about your kids

Granted, there are times when it will be impossible to avoid emergency discussions about pressing issues. And granted, you will need to set additional meetings to discuss the above items. But the main goal for your date nights is to enjoy your mate, have fun, and get to know each other on a more intimate level.

Here are additional ideas for your date night:

1. Discuss current events.
2. Read a book together.
3. Make something together, such as dinner or a craft.
4. See a movie, a theatrical production, or a concert.
5. Explore your city or neighborhood.
6. Go hiking, roller skating, or bowling.
7. Visit an art gallery.
8. Make dinner with friends.
9. Attend a county fair or other local event.
10. Go thrift shopping.
11. Work out together.

The ideas for a date night are endless. All you need is a little bit of creativity and a little bit of time. You can find many more ideas on the Internet. Focus on the Family is also a great source for ways to strengthen your marriage.

Spend regular devotional time together.

Do you and your mate spend time praying and reading the Bible together? According to my pastor, Andy Stanley, studies show that among couples who pray together the divorce rate is one in ten thousand instead of one out of two.[5] Devotional time can be a few moments each day and will give you a connecting point to talk about your lives. Again, there are numerous resources available online or at your local Christian bookstore.

Here are some questions to ask yourself as you develop the relational strategy for your mate:

- Do I make my mate feel loved and respected?
- Thirty years from now, what kind of memories do I want to make sure I have built with my mate?
- Do I help and support my mate in developing their calling and Blueprint for Life?
- Are there special places that I'd like to take my mate?
- Is there a desire my mate has expressed over the years, about something they'd like to do, or somewhere they'd like to go?
- Do I put others first before my mate?
- Do I know my mate's love language?
- How can I increase romance in our relationship?

YOUR KIDS

Step into their world.

There is no better way to express love and support to your child than to step into their world. This is one way to spend quality time in the right environment. It's one thing to take your children to do what you want to do; it's another thing entirely to encourage them by doing what *they* like to do.

In his book *Love Does*, author Bob Goff says that when he got married, he made a pact with his wife that when each of their children reached ten years old, they would get to go on a special trip with Dad. They called it the "ten-year-old adventure." The kids could pick any adventure that ignited their imagination or captured their curiosity. The best part was that every ten-year-old adventure included spontaneity. No planning, no preparation, and no worrying about details.

Bob's oldest daughter, Lindsey, turned ten first. Lindsey loved to do lots of things, but one of her favorites was having tea parties. She had heard about high tea provided for guests at some fancy hotels so she asked, "Dad, will you take me?" "You bet," he responded. Bob asked his daughter where she wanted to go to drink tea and eat fancy finger foods. When Lindsey said she didn't know, Bob suggested London. What could be better than having high tea in the city that the Queen of England calls her home?

Bob made flight arrangements and within a week, he and Lindsey were jetting through the friendly skies without a plan about where they would sleep, or what they would eat, because that is how you roll when you go on a three-day, ten-year-old adventure. Bob says the goal is to get to know one another better, and to experience an adventure, not a program.

Bob and Lindsey didn't wait to get over jetlag before they hit the ground running. They crammed all the fun they could in 72 hours. They visited Buckingham Palace, the Thames River, the Tower of London, and even the huge London Eye Ferris wheel. They ran through Hyde Park without shoes, munched on fish and chips, and toasted each other while drinking soda and lifting their pinky fingers. The last thing they did before hopping back on their flight was to have high tea at the Ritz. [6]

Bob Goff has done a great job of stepping into his kids' worlds and spending quality time with them in the right environment.

Make it a morning tradition.

Spending quality time with your kids doesn't mean you have to take time away to London or a faraway country. Instead you can make your relational strategy part of everyday life.

Deuteronomy 6:6–9 says, "These words which I command you today shall be in your heart. You shall teach them diligently to your children, and shall talk of them when you sit in your house, when you walk by the way, when you lie down, and when you rise up. You shall bind them as a sign on your hand, and they shall be as frontlets between your eyes. You shall write them on the doorposts of your house and on your gates."

As part of my daily relational strategy for my kids, each morning I ask myself, "What lesson can I leave with my kids today?" When I have settled on a topic, we talk about it during the fifteen-minute drive to school.

This morning I taught them about being exceptional, that God calls us to be different than the world. So I told them that if they see a piece of trash on the ground, they should pick it up. I added, "If you see someone standing alone without a friend on the playground, invite them to play. If other kids in your class are cheating, don't be like them. Instead, be exceptional for God."

Some days, we discuss one of the Proverbs because these are great lessons for how to live life in a God-honoring way. These morning lessons are part of how I want to leave a legacy for my kids and part of my relational strategy to spend quality time with them.

In chapter 8, we talked about how to enhance your inner circle, or relationship with Christ. And in this chapter, we have discussed how to develop a relational strategy for your mate and children. Now, in closing I'd like to share a few thoughts about friends and co-workers.

BE CAREFUL WHO YOU HITCH A RIDE WITH

Bob Goff tells an engaging story in *Love Does* that is a perfect anecdote about the truth that some people shouldn't be allowed in any of our circles. It doesn't mean that they are bad, but just that in order to honor God, we can't be close to them. When God has given us a calling, there are some people who just can't come along.

During college, Bob decided to hitchhike around the country. After hitching from San Diego to San Francisco, he got stuck on the side of the road for almost an entire day. After waiting for almost twenty-four hours, he was desperate to get going again, so he broke one unspoken rule that every hitchhiker knew: always ask where the driver is going rather than tell them where you want to go, to give them a chance to respond so you can check them out and see if they are safe. But after waiting for so long, Bob didn't keep this rule when a van pulled over.

I wasn't thinking about anything except getting farther north, so I climbed in before the van even had even come to a stop and threw my backpack in the space between the two front seats.

The guy driving looked about forty years old and had a huge beard. I was a little envious of his beard, actually, and imagined someday I could have that kind of wild man look. The windows weren't cracked, and it wasn't long before I caught wind of a toe curling body odor. I did a quick pit check to make sure I wasn't the source. This guy could have knocked over a water buffalo at fifty yards. No matter, I was moving again and that was all I cared about.

As we picked up speed, I noticed the dashboard was covered in rose petals. That's weird, I thought. Was this guy a florist? I was guessing no; or business must have been slow because there were no other flowers inside the hollow, creepy, windowless van. On the driver's side, on top of a different stash of flower petals, was a picture of guy's feet in a gold frame. If you're like me, you're probably thinking this is starting to get weird. *Why does someone have a picture of a dude's feet framed and set on top of flower*

YOUR BLUEPRINT FOR LIFE

petals? I wondered. My best guess was that the bearded, stinky guy wasn't a podiatrist. My weirdometer was pegged.

After fiddling with my backpack a little and looking out the window, I asked the guy, "So where are you headed?" No answer. This is precisely the reason I'd disciplined myself over the years to always ask someone where they are going before getting in with them. But on this occasion, I had . . . somehow forgotten my rule. I let a few long moments pass in the off chance he was just taking his time to answer. After a while, I figured that the first question didn't land so I offered in a cheery voice, "So where are you coming from today? Isn't it a beauty? I love this time of year, don't you?" No answer. Not a good sign.

I continued staring out the van window trying to put out an *I'm-not-freaked-out* vibe.

Then, without any prompting, the driver turned his head really slowly like the bad guys do in horror movies.

"Do you really want to know who I am?" he said in a voice covered with emphysema and evil. "Sure," I bandied, trying to keep the mood light. We were going to be in the van for a while. Might as well get to know each other, find areas of common interest . . . you know . . .

"I'm satan."

"Oh," I said, kind of wishing I had some holy water in my canteen.

I know it wasn't the most probing response, but it was all I could come up with at the time. It also seemed more succinct than, "Stinks to be you. How's the plan to destroy the world coming together?" "How's your mom? Do you have a mom?"

In reality, I was totally freaked out. If I had packed my Depends I would have strapped them on. I told satan, who I was surprised to note was smaller than me, to pull over and let me out of his van. While it was nice to be moving again, I figured he wasn't ultimately headed where I wanted to go.[7]

There are some people you should never hitch a ride with—and there are some people you should never allow in your circles. Granted, there are times when you can't control who you encounter each day, but you can determine who you allow to influence your life. You can determine if you can help someone live out God's calling for their life, and if they can be a positive influence in helping you with yours.

Some people think kicking someone out of your inner circles sounds callous. After all, Jesus would never do that, right? Wrong. He would. In our modern-day terminology, it's called having boundaries, and Jesus had a lot of them. He gave His most intimate time to men who wanted to go where He was going. He aligned Himself with those who had His Father's agenda in mind. Yes, He ate with sinners, but for those who were opposed to His plans, He didn't spend time wrangling with them.

Granted, you and I can't see into others' hearts like Jesus to know who we should let into our circles, but we have something powerful living inside us—the Holy Spirit—and we can ask God for discernment so that we can make wise choices in our closest relationships.

Prune That Relational Portfolio

Imagine a tree that has never been trimmed. As it grows, its branches become so heavy that the tree eventually breaks. A tree that has been pruned will be healthy and will not break under its

145

own weight. There are times in all of our lives when our relational portfolio is like a tree—it needs to be trimmed.

One man I know is a super networker. God has gifted him to be highly sociable. The problem is that this super-networker friend maintains so many relationships he can never go anywhere with his wife without someone interrupting to say hello. Or, he is so busy maintaining his relationships that he doesn't have time to spend quality time with her. His relational portfolio has crowded out his higher relational priorities.

If you are retired, you may have lots of extra time to maintain a large number of people in your relational portfolio. So, you may not need to prune it that often. But if you are a parent working outside the home, your relational portfolio will need to be smaller to make sure you have quality time for those closest to you. So, you may need to prune on a regular basis.

TIME TO REFLECT

As you think about the people who are currently in your relational circles, you may determine there are certain people missing or that you need to eliminate some relationships that are hindering your calling. In order to be a good steward of the time God has given you, you must be intentional about the relationships you cultivate. Because every relationship either supports or detracts from God's calling for your life.

Now that you have your circles identified, and you know not to push a stroller through the Magic Kingdom while talking on the phone, it's time to take a quiz about taking care of your body. Will it be A, B, C, or D? Your answers in the next chapter will help you develop a solid physical strategy to support your calling.

ETERNAL PERSPECTIVE SCRIPTURE

"For God is not unjust to forget your work and labor of love which you have shown toward His name, *in that* you have ministered to the saints, and do minister" (Heb. 6:10).

Chapter Ten

YOUR PHYSICAL STRATEGY

IMAGINE YOU ARE TAKING A trip. This is not just any trip; it's the vacation of a lifetime. The car is packed. The route is planned. The reservations are made. Everything is in place. As your family members fasten their seatbelts, anticipation fills the air. But as you turn the key, something else fills the air: smoke. It's the thick, blue kind that looks like it won't clear up any time soon. Next thing you know, you hear a loud rattling sound from under the hood and the engine suddenly stops. Vacation over.

Your body is like a car. It's your "transportation" for life. If you neglect or abuse it, just like a car, it's more likely to break down. You can understand God's blueprint for your life and implement all the other things we have talked about in this book, but if you don't take care of your body, you could end up on the side of the road. And, as one doctor friend says, "You can't serve God when you're sick."

There are many different viewpoints about taking care of our bodies. Here is a short quiz. Which viewpoint do you agree with most?

A. Since God says my days are numbered (Job 14:5), it doesn't matter how I treat my body. I am going to die when I die, and how I treat my body won't change that.

B. The spirit is more important than the body, so it doesn't matter if I care for my body. God wants me to focus on developing my spirit.

C. My body is very important. I care for it obsessively. I spend a substantial amount of time exercising each week, and I either rarely or never eat anything unhealthy. I guess you could say I worship my body.

D. Since my body is a temple of the Holy Spirit, it's important for me to care for it so I can carry out the work God has assigned to me. I know it's hard to serve God when you're sick.

Shana Schutte, a writer and speaker, asked her Facebook friends the above question. All of those who initially participated said they believe D is the right answer.

As the Ds piled up, Shana said she started to wonder if there is a gap between our "theology" and reality on this topic. Suddenly a man commented, "[I believe] D in theory, although wavering back and forth between B and D is closer to actual practice."

Suddenly others admitted they also struggle with taking care of their bodies. They agree with D, but what they *do* is contrary to their beliefs. Given disease and obesity rates in our country—even in the church—it's a strong indication that we may "talk the talk but not walk the walk."

Which attitude describes you most? And are your actions and what you say you believe in agreement? If not, why? What is holding you back from becoming all you can be for God?

I am definitely not pointing a finger, as I have a lot to learn about health and I can always become more diligent about exercise. But do we truly believe that our bodies are temples of the Holy Spirit and that we are called to care for them so we can fulfill our God-given calling?

Okay, let's take a closer look at each of these perspectives.

Since God says my days are numbered (Job 14:5), it doesn't matter how I treat my body. I am going to die when I die, and how I treat my body won't change that.

In his book *Anxious for Nothing*, Dr. John MacArthur wrote:

We live in a day when people are in a panic to lengthen their lives. They have an excessive interest in vitamins, health spas, diet, and exercise. God, however, has previously determined how long we shall live. Job 14:5 says of man, "His days are determined, the number of his months is with You; and his limits You have set so that he cannot pass." Does that mean we should disregard sensible advice about our diet and exercise? Of course not: It will increase the quality of our lives, but there's no guarantee about the quantity. When I exercise and eat right, my body and brain work better and I feel more energetic, but I'm not going to kid myself that by jogging in the neighborhood every day and eating hefty quantities of complex carbohydrates that I'm going to force God to let me live longer.[1]

I agree with Dr. MacArthur. We cannot *lengthen* our lives, but we can negatively affect the *quality* of our lives and our ability to serve Christ well if we abuse our bodies.

If you talk to anyone who is connected to an oxygen tank because of all their years smoking, or someone who cannot get out of bed because they are dealing with depression due to exhaustion, they will tell you that all of their energy and time is invested in dealing with the disease of their body. Disease is consuming, and it demands full attention.

As we think about abusing our bodies, abuse isn't just defined as drinking, taking drugs, or eating too much junk food. Abuse can happen over a long period of time as we simply neglect our bodies. Just like a car, our bodies require regular maintenance to perform optimally.

God has designed our bodies amazingly well. They will sustain years of abuse before disease develops. So for a time, we may think we are getting a free ride; but we must remember that just as God created every living thing to operate within natural laws, our bodies are the same. They function optimally when we treat them how God designed them to be treated.

The spirit is more important than the body, so it doesn't matter if I care for my body. God wants me to focus on developing my spirit.

Some people emphasize the importance of the spirit and neglect their body. But just like a car with multiple parts that work together, our soul (mind, will, and emotions), spirit, and body work together too.

Imagine if I said, "Well, I don't really need to take care of the tires on my car because it's the engine that matters." If I neglect the tires, no matter how well I care for the engine, one day I could be stranded on the side of the road going nowhere for God. When we neglect our bodies, we risk negatively affecting every area of our lives.

My body is very important. I care for it obsessively. I spend a substantial amount of time exercising each week, and I either rarely or never eat anything unhealthy. I guess you could say I worship my body.

Janice is a self-professed exercise fanatic. She must weight train, jog, and swim for several hours every day or she feels anxious or depressed. When she goes out to dinner, she mentally runs a calorie counter to determine how much exercise she will need to do to burn off what she has eaten. Even when she was pregnant she continued to exercise strenuously despite the concern of others. Her addiction to exercise started in her early twenties, and although she knows that she goes overboard, she isn't sure how to stop.

For some people health is like a drug; it's an obsession. Instead of overeating and neglecting their bodies, they place an extreme amount of focus on physically improving themselves. They become so focused with keeping their weight down and how they look that they make an idol out of their body. This goes against God's developing blueprint for our lives because one's blueprint is about glorifying God and not focusing on ourselves.

Since my body is the temple of the Holy Spirit, it's important for me to care for it so I can carry out the work God has assigned for me. I know it's hard to serve God when you're sick.

First Corinthians 6:19–20 says, "Your body is the temple of the Holy Spirit. . . . you are not your own? For you were bought at a price; therefore glorify God in your body."

Granted, the context of this scripture is about not giving oneself to a prostitute. But the implication is that our bodies are holy and to be revered. For this reason, how we maintain them is not a personal preference; it's a spiritual issue.

In an audio message titled "How Much Does God Want Me to Care for My Physical Body?" pastor John Piper offers the following, which may explain why so many say it's important to take care of our bodies, but do the opposite:

The reason people are unhealthy is because they're enslaved. They are enslaved to laziness, and they are enslaved to food. So they eat too much and they exercise too little. And they have heart attacks and get diabetes. And God would consider that a spiritual issue.

So we should strive spiritually. What did Paul mean when he said, "I will not be enslaved by anything"? He meant, "Christ is your master!" . . . So we should fight against anything that makes us unhealthy. If overeating makes us unhealthy, fight it by the Spirit. If laziness and lack of exercise makes us unhealthy, fight it with the power of the Holy Spirit. That is, believing the promises of God, praying down the Holy Spirit, and then biting the bullet and denying ourselves.[2]

Note that Dr. Piper says we need to fight physical battles with faith. In her book *Made to Crave*, Lysa TerKeurst tells about how she learned to do this; but until then, exercise just made her want to cry.

So she would stand in front of the bathroom mirror and lament over which pants would best hide her bulge. She cried out to God and tried to convince herself that she just needed to rise above the vain issue of worrying about her weight. After all, wasn't she at the stage of life when being fit was kind of unrealistic?

She had birthed three children and was too busy running her kids here and there to exercise. She also told herself that she should be more concerned about her spirituality than her pant size. She should unconditionally accept herself like God unconditionally accepted her.

Deep down, Lysa knew her extra weight had *everything* to do with having a lack of self-control. And, even though exercise made her want to cry, she did something interesting: she invited God into her exercise routine.

> At first I could only slowly jog from one mailbox to another—in a neighborhood where houses are close together, thank you very much. Slowly, I started to see little evidences of progress. The key word here is *slowly*.
>
> Every day I asked God to give me the strength to stick with it this time. I'd tried so many other times and failed after only a few weeks. The more I made running about spiritual growth and discipline, the less I focused on the weight. Each lost pound was not a quest to get skinny but evidence of obedience to God.
>
> One day, I went out [for] my version of a run and God clearly spoke to my heart. I often spent my exercise time talking with God, but today a clear command from God rumbled in my heart: "Run until you can't take another step. Do it not in your own strength but in Mine. Every time you want to stop, pray for that struggling friend you just challenged not to give up and take your own advice—don't stop until I tell you to."
>
> There have been many other times when God has given me clear directives to do things but never one that was this physically demanding. I had a record up to that point of running three miles, which I thought was quite stellar. For me, three miles seemed like a marathon. So, maybe God wanted me to run just slightly past the three-mile marker and rejoice in relying on His strength to do so. But as I reached that point in my run, my heart betrayed my aching body and said, "Keep going."
>
> Each step thereafter, I had to pray and rely on God. The more I focused on running toward God, the less I thought about my desire to stop. And this verse from the Psalms came to life, "My

flesh and my heart may fail, but God is the strength of my heart and my portion forever" (73:26).

As I ran that day, I connected with God on a different level. I experienced what it meant to absolutely require God's faith to see something through. How many times have I claimed to be a woman of faith but rarely lived a life requiring faith? That day, God didn't have me stop until I ran 8.6 miles.

Hear me out here. It was my legs that took every step. It was *my* energy being used. It was *my* effort that took me from one mile to three to five to seven to 8.6. But it was *God's strength* replacing my excuses step by step by step.

For a mailbox-to-mailbox, crying-when-she-thought-of-exercising-allergic-to-physical-discipline kind of girl, it was a modern-day miracle. I broke through the "I-can't" barrier and expanded the horizons of my reality. Was it hard? Yes. Was it tempting to quit? Absolutely. Could I do this in my own strength? Never. But this really wasn't about running. It was about realizing the power of God taking over my complete weakness.[3]

As we take this journey, I want to give you some guidelines to help you improve your physical health, so you can experience God's calling for your life in its fullness. But it's important to start at the beginning, and the beginning is committing your physical blueprint to Christ. I invite you to pray the following prayer.

Lord Jesus, I submit my physical body and health to You. God, there are days when I don't want to do what is best for the temple You have given me. Please give me strength. I ask You to remind me that taking care of my body isn't just an issue of personal prefer-ence; it's a spiritual issue. It's a way I serve and glorify You. Like all gifts that You have given me, please help me to take care of my temple so I can fulfill Your blueprint for my life.

———

Okay, here we go! We are off to a great start, and I am glad you are with me on this journey. Let's begin by taking a look at six key areas that will lay a foundation for great physical health.

EXERCISE AND FITNESS

Maybe you're like Lysa and exercise makes you want to cry. Or maybe you enjoy it. Regardless, any good physical strategy includes exercise and fitness.

Before you roll your eyes and throw this book in the trash, let me encourage you . . . exercise doesn't have to take hours and hours of time every day to be beneficial.

I like to spend a couple of hours, three days a week, at the gym lifting weights. On three opposite days, I complete thirty minutes of cardio. Sometimes I run on the treadmill, and some days I use the StairMaster. There are days when getting to the gym is difficult due to my schedule, but I never regret going after I walk out the door to drive home. My mind is clearer, I feel energized, and it strengthens my body.

You may choose a different exercise plan. Regardless of which plan you choose, it's important to just choose one. And remember, the best kind of exercise is the kind you will do. So pick something you enjoy.

According to the Mayo Clinic, exercise also does the following:

1. Exercise boosts energy.

Like me, maybe you know what it's like to have a busy schedule. Maybe you are thinking, *I don't have time to exercise.* Let me encourage you: you don't have time *not* to.

Exercise will actually multiply your time by increasing your energy level because it will deliver oxygen and nutrients to your tissues and help your cardiovascular system work more efficiently. Then you'll have more energy and clarity to devote to your calling. Who couldn't use a little more of that?

2. Exercise controls weight.

There are all kinds of gimmicks on television, on radio, and at the grocery checkout line trying to convince you to choose a fast and easy way to lose weight. But the healthiest, best way to lose weight is just the old-fashioned way. You just need to eat right and get up and move!

This idea is nothing new; no doubt you've already heard that exercise aids in weight loss. And the greater your physical activity level, the more calories you will burn.

Experts also say that muscle helps to burn fat, so people with more muscle mass burn more calories even when they are at rest. So why not try lifting weights, bench-pressing your little boy, or carrying a heavy rock up and down the street?

3. Exercise combats health conditions and diseases.

If you are worried about heart disease or want to prevent high blood pressure, being active boosts high-density lipoprotein (HDL), or "good" cholesterol, and decreases unhealthy triglycerides. This is good news, because it will help keep your blood flowing smoothly, to decrease your risk of cardiovascular diseases. Not only that, but regular physical activity can help you prevent or manage a wide range of health problems and concerns, including stroke, metabolic syndrome, type 2 diabetes, depression, certain types of cancer, arthritis, and falls.

4. Exercise improves mood.

I have always believed that a lot of people who feel blue would be greatly helped by just doing a little physical activity. Come to find out, I was right. God designed us so that physical activity stimulates brain activity. Just a twenty-minute walk increases feel-good hormones in the brain to a significant degree.[4] Feeling blue? Get up and move!

Setting Fitness Goals

Some people exercise sporadically, or just every now and then. But consistency and frequency are important keys to good health. As you exercise, it's important to set goals for maximum weight lifted, distance run, and proficiency. You can also include goals for your body weight, clothing size, waist size, and muscle tone.

Here are some practical things you can do to reach your fitness goals:

Start slow.

Some people try to do too much when they first begin an exercise plan. Then they get discouraged and quit. It's better to start slow and increase your activity level. A gradual approach to fitness will keep you motivated and prevent injuries. But before you begin, consult your doctor.

Write it down!

In addition to being a good reminder of what you've done at each workout, a written log will help you track progress. Before you start your program, write down your goals. You'll be surprised at how this will help keep you on track.

Get a workout buddy.

Maybe you have heard that there is strength in numbers. It's true! I work out regularly with one of my best friends. Accountability will help you stay consistent. Some people choose to hire a trainer from a local gym. No matter how you do it, finding a workout buddy is a good idea.

Put it on the schedule.

I firmly believe that if something is on your calendar, there is a much greater chance that you will get it done. Just like you schedule a time to get out of bed each day, schedule a time to exercise. A routine often makes it easier to stick with an exercise program.

Go a different direction.

For a lot of people, doing the same exercise or taking the same route can get boring. If you run or walk, you can check out new neighborhoods, tracks, or parks. When you change scenery, it can add interest to your routine and keep you from getting bored.

Bring your tunes.

For a lot of people, listening to music is a good distraction. Some people like to choose a particular group of songs for their iPod to listen to during their workout. They use faster tunes to boost the intensity of their workout and calmer music to help cool down.

Change it up.

There are a host of various types of exercise you can do to stay interested. There's yoga for stretching and balance, running, walking, jogging, bicycling, and weight training. Cross training, circuit training, or combining a variety of exercises is a great way to boost metabolism. In addition to your regular exercise routine, you can park farther away from the grocery store entrance, take the stairs at work, or walk, instead of drive, to meet your friend for coffee.

Drink up the H_2O!

Remember that your body is 70 percent water. If you haven't had enough to drink, your workout may fall below expectations.

Don't become distracted.

In today's fast-paced society, it can be tempting to put exercise at the bottom of your to-do list. Do you have a commitment to keep exercise in your daily schedule no matter distractions or scheduling challenges? If you think of exercise as as much of a commitment as your job, brushing your teeth, or sleeping, it will be easier to keep it as a priority.

DIET

Just like a car needs gas, your body needs fuel. But not just any fuel. Your organs need specific vitamins and minerals to perform optimally. Even if you keep your stomach full, you could still be starving your body of the vital nutrients it needs to function. Or, you could become thinner by following a fad diet, but could also starve your body of nutrients. Your goal is not just to watch calories, but also to consume healthy nutrients.

When God made the seed-bearing plants, He saw that they were good and told Adam and Eve that they could eat from any of these good plants (Gen. 2:16). In Genesis 1:29, God said, "See, I have given you every herb that yields seed which is on the face of all the earth, and every tree whose fruit yields seed; to you it shall be for food."

One thing that I appreciate about God is that He never does anything without a reason. He didn't just make fruit because it tastes good or because He knew we would like it. He created it because it will help us stay healthy. He didn't make broccoli to irritate us. He made it for us to enjoy and with specific chemicals to help our bodies run well and fight disease.

Your physical strategy should include learning and understanding God's plan for food. Most doctors agree that eating a good amount of fruits, vegetables, and other healthy foods is a good idea.

Some people who want to lose weight monitor the size or frequency of meals. Others choose foods with a high nutrient-to-calorie ratio. Whatever plan you adopt, remember to say no to the harmful and yes to the beneficial.

REST

In the Bible, God highly values rest. He says that for six days we should do our work, then we should rest on the seventh day. But rest isn't just about keeping the Sabbath; it's about keeping a balanced lifestyle.

As a busy business professional, this can be challenging; and when you are really excited about pursuing your calling, it can also be challenging. But I have discovered that the busier I am, the more important it is to build rest into my schedule.

I mentioned I launched a new company called iDisciple. In a short period of time, a small team has accomplished amazing things, but the pace was frantic for a while. Setting up a new business takes a lot of focus and work.

During this period of time I was reminded there may be seasons of intensity to do what God has called you to do. But no one can sustain pushing too hard for too long. Our bodies were not made for it. If we do not build rest into our schedules, we will eventually experience burnout.

People who avoid burnout and succeed in the long run know how to pace themselves. We have to understand how to plan within our God-given boundaries. That means getting sleep, for example. It also means managing expectations for your calling including when and how you will reach the stepping-stones I mentioned earlier in the book. If your vision is bigger than your ability to accomplish it in a particular time period, you may push yourself too hard and experience burnout. Your time and resources must match your goals. If they do not, you may end up exhausted, fatigued, and maybe even depressed. This is what Pastor Tommy Nelson, senior pastor of Denton Bible Church in Denton, Texas, experienced.

Nelson was a high-profile pastor of a thriving church with big impact. For years, he taught an early morning class four days a week, conducted a staff Bible study, led three weekly men's studies, as well as the largest singles' study in the country. He also preached on Sundays and counseled church members. On top of all that, his writing and speaking opportunities were flourishing and he traveled many times during the year to promote his *Song of Solomon* series for couples. It wasn't unusual for him to teach thirteen to twenty times per week.

But then his lifestyle and schedule caught up with him.

Nelson started battling insomnia and aches in his body that felt like electrical currents shooting through his muscles. Physicians thought he might have allergies but said they couldn't do anything to help.

After wrestling with sleepless nights and constant aches and pains, Nelson shut down emotionally. He said he fell into a "black hole." He felt an emotional numbness, a nothingness. It was a darkness he hadn't ever experienced in his life. He couldn't understand how he could be experiencing something so difficult, because he was enjoying life, doing what he was called to do. In fact, he was so excited about serving God that he would wake up in the middle of the night, excited about what he would do in the morning for God. He saw doctor after doctor, but no one could find anything physically wrong.

Finally, a member of his church suggested that Nelson might be depressed, so he visited a psychiatrist. In minutes, the doctor confirmed the church member's statement.

"He listened to me for about fifteen minutes and said, 'You're garden variety. You're nothing problematic,'" said Nelson. The doctor told Nelson he sees guys just like him a couple of times a day.

The psychiatrist explained that when someone is in a constant state of busyness, when they are always in go-mode, that adrenaline is constantly on. It's like being in overdrive. When this happens, adrenaline reduces brain serotonin levels, which leads to depression.

While the diagnosis was simple, Nelson couldn't just pop a pill for an easy fix. Instead, the doctor prescribed rest and relaxation and several months off from work to rebuild the serotonin levels in his brain. This meant he had to reduce his workload and cut out the teaching and speaking opportunities he enjoyed so much.

Now Nelson says he's just a "regular old preacher." "I had to cut back and start making my stuff real quality and strategic rather than running so hard and getting by on four or five hours of sleep."

It took about a year before Nelson started feeling like himself again. Now, he is a big advocate of keeping life in balance.

"There's a natural happiness to life when you're rightly related to it—just a joy—especially as a Christian; but when you are going through this, you can't feel it," Nelson said. "I think when you've finished going through something like that, you have a sensitivity to how you feel that you never had before. You don't take for granted just feeling good. It makes you very happy about the simple things like your mental health, because if something is wrong with your mind, it really scares you. So, whenever you get rid of it, you realize that the happiest thing in the world is just being you."[5]

You must include regular rest as a part of your physical strategy. In our culture rest is optional, but God created us to live balanced lives. Even when we are doing something we love, we need to build rest into our schedules. For me, this means that I set aside time each week when I can disengage from my commitments. I may take my family to the beach, watch a football game, or spend time having fun with my son.

Give your God-given calling and career your best, but keep it in balance so you don't end up stranded on the side of the road. What plan will you implement in your physical strategy so you can disengage and experience rest?

SLEEP

If you Google "I can't sleep," more than 108 million results will pop up. It's no surprise. Open Facebook in the middle of the night and you will discover there are a lot of insomniacs out there.

The National Sleep Foundation conducted a survey of 1,004 Americans and learned that the vast majority—63 percent—do not get the eight hours recommended by experts for good health. As much as 40 percent indicated that several times a month they are so sleepy during the day that it interferes with their daily activities. Nearly half reported that they have driven while drowsy, and 20 percent say they have actually fallen asleep while behind the wheel.[6]

Somewhere along the way, we have lost the perception that sleep is a necessity for good health, and we tend to consider it negotiable or a luxury instead. If you want good health and optimal performance—whether achieving at work or just staying awake during your prayer time—you need a strategy for getting a good night's sleep. You should set a time for going to bed and work your schedule back from there. People's sleep needs can vary, so you might do well to have a certain number of hours as a goal. Pay attention to the impact that certain foods and drinks can have on restful sleep—and the way evening snacks can alter sleep patterns.

If you have a hard time sleeping, here are tips for getting a good night's sleep.

Set a regular bedtime. Going to bed at the same time every night isn't just for kids. It's for adults too. When you keep a regular sleep schedule and choose a time when you normally feel tired to go to bed, it can keep you from feeling fatigued during the day. Even if it's difficult, try not to break this routine during the weekend. If for some reason you want to change your bedtime, rather than doing it all at once, help your body adjust by slowly changing the time you go to bed in small increments.

Wake up at the same time every day. Even though it's not possible for most people, it's best to wake up without an alarm. If you need an alarm clock to wake, going to bed earlier is a good idea. As with your bedtime, try to maintain your regular wake-time even on weekends.

Nap to make up for lost sleep. Just as going to bed at the same time every night isn't just for children, taking naps isn't just for kids either. If you feel tired during the day, you can take a short nap rather than sleeping in late. This way, you can gain energy without inter-rupting your regular sleep schedule. And napping won't cause you to develop insomnia and wake up during the night either.

Keep your room free of noisy electronic devices. If you have a cell phone or other electronic device that makes noises during the night and you need to keep it on, place it in another room so that your sleep is not interrupted.

Fight after-dinner drowsiness. Sometimes drowsiness can set in after a meal. If this happens to you, it can be helpful to get up and move following a meal. You can go for a walk, or even do something easier like wash the dishes, do laundry, or mop the kitchen floor. This will prevent you from going to bed too early and disrupting your sleep schedule.

If you have tried the tips above and are still having a difficult time sleeping, you may have a sleep disorder that requires profes-sional treatment. Some people get into the habit of taking sleeping pills but then later have a difficult time giving them up. As one of my friends once discovered, they can be very addicting. So rather than resort to consistently taking medication, consider scheduling a visit with a sleep doctor instead.

Appearance

In his book *Pinnochio Parenting*, Dr. Chuck Bisango investigates the lies that parents tell their kids, such as Santa Claus is real, you can be anything you want to be—and looks don't matter; it's what is on the inside that counts.

Though we live in a world that emphasizes physical attractiveness, it would be unwise and ungodly to develop a life that is only skin deep. But it would be wise to make the most of the assets you have been given to support God's blueprint for your life. This will affect how you feel about yourself and how others perceive you.

Imagine if I, as a businessman, showed up to work every day unshaven, wearing shorts and a Hawaiian shirt. How do you think others would perceive me? Would this affect my ability to make business deals? First impressions do make an impression whether we want them to or not. Additionally, the way we look needs to match our callings.

For example, I once heard of a man who sold insurance to farmers. Whenever he went on a business call, he didn't wear a suit and tie; he wore work boots and jeans. He figured that the farmers wouldn't be able to relate to him if he was dressed like he was going to the office.

If improving or changing certain aspects of your appearance will help you fulfill God's calling for your life, it might be worth doing so.

Have you considered how your overall appearance affects your success? Does appearance matter? What about your wardrobe? Are there certain outfits you want to be sure are up-to-date to aid your career goals? Do you have a plan for refreshing your wardrobe?

What's your overall plan for improving your physical appearance to support God's calling for your life?

MENTAL/EMOTIONAL

Just as your physical condition affects your performance, your mental and emotional state also has the ability to propel you toward your goals or leave you stranded on the side of the road. For some people, emotions rarely warrant a second thought. For many people, mental or emotional hindrances can be debilitating. Almost everyone can identify one or two areas in which they can make improvements to better their quality of life. For example, an ordinary fear of flying is not uncommon. But if it causes you to avoid certain trips or pass up opportunities that serve your calling, it's something you'll want to pray about and seek professional help for.

Are there any fears that might be limiting your potential? Are there painful or unpleasant memories from the past that are holding you back? Are you experiencing guilt and shame? If you want to get help, help is available through counseling services and churches across the country. You can also search the Internet for a licensed Christian professional in your area.

Now that we have taken a look at how you can develop a physical strategy, let's take a look at how you can develop a solid financial strategy too.

ETERNAL PERSPECTIVE SCRIPTURE

"Each one will receive his own reward according to his own labor"
(1 Cor. 3:8).

Chapter Eleven

YOUR FINANCIAL STRATEGY

I HAD A SURREAL MOMENT ON my fortieth birthday, and I sometimes still wonder if it was just a dream. My wife and I rented a
yacht to celebrate, and we were sailing from Martha's Vineyard to
Nantucket and Newport.

While lounging on the deck one afternoon, I got a call on my cell
phone from a client. After a short discussion, my partner, Eric, and I
agreed to sell stock we had in the client's company. In just a few minutes, we made a multimillion-dollar profit.

That's when it occurred to me. *This is as good as it is ever going
to get.* After all, I was on a one-hundred-foot yacht looking out over
Nantucket on my birthday with a shrimp cocktail in hand. What
could be better? But even in that moment of excitement, I knew
I had to be careful or I could experience a serious downfall. Not
because of the possibility of losing the money, but because I could
live a wasted and unfulfilled life by making money my goal instead
of living for God. I knew if I wanted to live a satisfying life and make
an impact for Christ, I had to invest my financial resources in what
truly mattered . . . I had to use the money God had entrusted to me
for *His purposes.*

In that moment, the financial principles I'd like to share with
you in this chapter became paramount in my life. Through them,
I knew I could serve God, keep my finances in balance to support
my calling, *and* make a big eternal impact. Could there be anything
better than that?

Before I share these life-changing principles, I'd like to share six common, false beliefs about money.

"The only way I will be happy is to be rich." A lot of people think being rich will solve their problems and make them happy. But would you say that Bernie Madoff, Tiger Woods, Michael Vick, and Lindsey Lohan are happy? I'm not saying they aren't, but I am saying being rich has always been a pretty poor guarantor of happiness. Not only that, it hasn't prevented train wrecks for any of these people. In some cases, there's even an opposite relationship between wealth and happiness. Sometimes, the richer they are, the harder they fall.

Rich people aren't rich because they have treasure. They're rich—or internally fulfilled—because of *how they allocate their treasure.*

To explore my theory, let me introduce you to the wealthiest man who ever lived. Forget Bill Gates or Warren Buffet. Let's go all the way to the top. According to many respected authorities, the richest man who ever lived has held the number one spot for more than three thousand years—and no one has surpassed him yet. Nor is there anyone in recorded history whose wealth has been greater. He was King Solomon of Israel.

Not only is Solomon believed to have had more wealth than all the other examples we could choose, he also wrote extensively about his experiences with wealth. So we have an excellent case study of the relationship between being rich and being happy.

One of the most valuable aspects of Solomon's life is that we get insight into the thought lives of the mega-rich. Solomon shared his unedited and raw emotions for the world to see. Unabashedly, he recounted the extreme pleasure of fulfilling his wildest dreams— and he mourned the reality that some of his most basic needs and deepest longings couldn't be met with money.

According to some of our best historical documents, King Solomon enjoyed every form of luxury imaginable, and he spent his time however he wished. Yet somehow the secret to happiness eluded him. He had wealth, health, family, and religion. But when you read his accounts, it's obvious that the richest man in the world was also one of the poorest in terms of happiness. No doubt today a doctor would put him on anti-depressants. To put Solomon's life into perspective, let's compare his lifestyle and net worth in today's terms.

Although it's hard to translate the value of Solomon's gold into modern US currency, most scholars estimate his base annual salary was more than half a billion dollars. In addition, ancient records indicate gifts of gold from neighboring countries totaling nearly one hundred thousand pounds. At today's prices, let's just say that would be somewhere in the billions.

Solomon also owned twelve thousand horses, fourteen hundred chariots, and vast stores of ivory, spices, and precious stones. He controlled palaces and cities, and he collected a portion of all trade between countries to the north and south. He was loaded. And he did not withhold his heart from any pleasure. He lavished every conceivable perk on himself.

It's hard to picture what it was really like to be Solomon. If anyone held the dream of happiness in the palm of his hand, it was him. So imagine the angst he must have felt when he realized he was anything but happy. Instead, he was in agony and despair. He wrote,

"I hated life, because the work that is done under the sun was grievous to me. All of it is meaningless, a chasing after the wind. I hated all the things I had toiled for under the sun" (Eccl. 2:17–18 NIV). What a terrific object lesson Solomon's life is for us! It's a perfectly crafted message that shows that "rich" does not equal "happy."

The life of Solomon also illustrates what I call "the Law of Fulfillment." This law states that we'll be fulfilled when we expend our time, talent, and treasure for the good of others and for God's glory. This has certainly been true in my life. You don't have to be wealthy to be rich. Richness is embodied in the beautiful and simple phrase spoken by our Lord Jesus: "It is more blessed to give than to receive" (Acts 20:35).

"THE ONLY WAY I WILL BE SUCCESSFUL IS TO HAVE A LOT OF MONEY." I mentioned earlier that God's value system is radically different from ours. Often, His ways are opposite from ours. For example, the first will be last and the last will be first (Matt. 20:16); to be great in His kingdom, we must become servants (Mark 9:35); the proud will be humbled; the humble will be exalted (Matt. 23:12); those who mourn are blessed (Matt. 5:4); only when we are weak are we in a position to experience His strength (2 Cor. 12:9); and to truly live, we must die to ourselves (Rom. 6:8).

These upside-down ways of looking at the world remind us we shouldn't be surprised that God doesn't define success like we do.

For example, God doesn't consider the CEO of a Fortune 500 company a success just because of his position and salary. A $120,000 Mercedes doesn't impress Him. He doesn't care if you make a name for yourself, make a lot of money, or make it onto Oprah. Instead, He says you are successful when you know Him, glorify Him, and fulfill your calling with excellence.

Perhaps the best illustration of God's perspective about success is His own Son. Jesus wasn't born into a wealthy family with earthly fanfare; He was born in a stable among farm animals. His father was a hard-working carpenter in a small town. And, when Jesus chose His disciples, He didn't select the wealthy or those the world would consider successful. He chose common fishermen, a despised tax collector, and other ordinary guys. Even after His reputation grew and people wanted to crown Him as their leader, Christ chose the cross instead, a humiliating and disgraceful instrument of torture.

In spite of humble beginnings and a shameful death, Jesus was amazingly successful because He completed all that His Father sent Him to do (John 17:4). God's value system is not like ours at all. Will you live for what God values rather than what the world values—or will you define success according to the world's ways?

"I MUST HOARD MY MONEY TO BE SAFE." There is no guarantee that if you hoard money and carefully manage it that you will always have it. There have been a couple of times in my life that my net worth has been more than $100 million. In my early forties, I naively thought this would last forever. Then the dot-com bubble burst, and much of what I had in my portfolio was lost. What I regret most is that I didn't invest that money in God's kingdom. It just sat in my brokerage account and made no impact for Christ, then boom! Without warning, it disappeared! Even though it is wise to save, we cannot rely on money to provide safety for us; and to think we can protect ourselves by trusting in it is foolish. We are to trust in God, not in money. This is why it's important to invest it wisely in the things that will make a difference for Christ and glorify Him while we have the chance.

These first three false beliefs I just described make an idol out of money. People who chase after wealth because they believe it will make them happy, make them successful, or inoculate them from trouble are the ones who will say no to God when He calls them to take a risk in their calling. Remember, "No one can serve two masters; for either he will hate the one and love the other, or else he will be loyal to the one and despise the other. You cannot serve God and mammon [money]" (Matt. 6:24). Don't let the deceitfulness of wealth cause you to live an unfruitful life (Matt. 13:22). Don't serve money; serve God with your money instead.

"I'M NOT GOOD WITH MONEY AND I NEVER WILL BE." According to Kachina Myers, a New York City professional who specializes in helping clients with financial issues, there is a big problem with believing the above statement because it turns managing money and financial knowledge into something that is unchangeable, like having black hair and blue eyes, rather than a skill. Myers said, "Money management is like cooking, or fixing a car, or anything else you can learn. But if you tell yourself you're simply not good at it, you're less likely to take steps to learn the basics you need to be financially healthy."[1]

The Bible says, "His divine power has given to us all things that pertain to life and godliness" (2 Peter 1:3). This includes the ability to handle money God's way. In fact, the Bible contains more than two thousand verses dedicated to helping us deal with money how God intended.

"MY FINANCES HAVE NOTHING TO DO WITH MY FAITH." Many people believe they can divorce their faith from their finances, but they are interwoven and one affects the other. In his book *The Treasure Principle,* Randy Alcorn wrote, "We may try to divorce our faith in our finances, but God sees them as inseparable."[2]

How we handle our finances and the other resources God has entrusted to us—if we share with others and give to God's purposes—reveals a lot about what we believe about Christ, His involvement in our lives, and His willingness to care for us. If I am unwilling to sacrifice for Him by sacrificially giving, what does that say about my belief that He will care for me? What does it say about my love for my brothers and sisters? What does it say about my fear, pride, or selfishness? What I do with my money says a lot about my heart condition.

Scripture also says all the resources we have been entrusted with were given to us by God. They all belong to Him, so our finances have *everything* to do with our faith. For example . . .

- The earth is the LORD's, and everything in it, the world, and all who live in it. (Ps. 24:1 NIV)
- "The silver is mine and the gold is mine," declares the LORD Almighty. (Hag. 2:8 NIV)
- Remember the LORD your God, for it is he who gives you the ability to produce wealth. (Deut. 8:18 NIV)

It all belongs to Him because it all came from Him. So when we manage our money and resources well, we are managing His money and resources. When we give to a church or ministry, we aren't giving our money; we are giving His money. God has just given us the blessed privilege of managing His money. What does the way you handle your financial resources say about your faith?

"GOD WANTS ME TO BE HAPPY, AND SINCE I CAN'T TAKE IT WITH ME, I AM GOING TO SPEND EVERY DOLLAR I GET." Imagine you were just hired to work on a crew to build a house. During your interview, your new boss says, "Make sure you show up on the job with your tool box and all the tools you need to do the job." But you don't listen and you show up on Monday morning with an empty toolbox.

If you spend every dime you get on your own wants and pleasures, you will be greatly limited in your ability to build God's kingdom. It's like trying to build a house without tools because money is a tool to build God's kingdom and make an eternal impact.

Jesus echoed this truth in Luke 16:9 when He said, "I tell you, use worldly wealth to gain friends for yourselves, so that when it is gone, you will be welcomed into eternal dwellings" (NIV). Amazing! This scripture reveals that while we can't take our money with us, we can send it on ahead of us to make a difference in heaven.

Some people think that living with eternity in mind by using one's money to gain eternal rewards is selfish, but it's clear Christ is inviting us to store up treasure in heaven. He is even *commanding* that we do.

Do you identify with any of the above attitudes? If so, I invite you to pray and ask the Lord to give you His perspective. Then, go out and glorify Him and make Him known with what He has provided for you!

Now that we have taken a look at these wrong attitudes, let's take a look at those life-changing principles I mentioned at the beginning of the chapter.

GOD'S PURPOSES FOR YOUR MONEY

I invite you to start a conversation about money in a crowded room and watch what happens. Some people will become angry because their neighbor has more; some will get excited at the thought of getting more; and some will feel anxiety because they don't know how they will pay their electric bill this month—but all have been given an allotment from God.

What you do with your allotment is an act of obedience to Christ, and it's also how you serve and glorify Him. It's also one way you can support your calling to make that eternal impact like we talked about. Remember, if you don't honor God with your money, then your relationship with Christ will never be what it should.

Which brings me to God's purposes for your money: giving, provisions, and abundance.

Giving

I'm sure you can think of a lot of things to do with your money. You can go to the movies, spend it on a new suit, or go out to your favorite restaurant. But one thing God definitely wants you to do with some of it is to *give*.

When some people hear the word *give* they groan. I get it. I know some misguided church leaders have manipulated people into giving by promising they will receive immediate blessings in return, and others have guilted people into giving. Regardless of how you feel about giving, it's important to remember that giving wasn't invented by the church, another religious organization, or a pastor. Giving was God's idea. It all started with Him. Through giving we can demonstrate our love for Him, build His kingdom, glorify Him, and make an eternal impact.

There are two specific ways God wants us to give, the first of which is demanded off the top of our income, no matter how much or little it may be.

Tithes

In Malachi 3:8–10, God told the Israelites that they were robbing Him. He said, "Will a man rob God? Yet you have robbed Me! But you say, 'In what way have we robbed You?' In tithes and offerings. You are cursed with a curse, for you have robbed Me, *even* this whole nation. Bring all the tithes into the storehouse, that there may be food in My house. And try Me now in this."

There are some things in life that are optional, like brushing your teeth, taking a shower, or watering your lawn. It's clear through this scripture that tithing isn't optional.

The word *tithe* literally means "tenth" and it's to be given to support a local church or other ministry that carries out God's kingdom work to glorify Him and make Him known.

Since all the financial resources we have belong to God, it's pretty cool and gracious of Him that we get to keep 90 percent of what He gives us—and He only asks us to give 10 percent back!

You need to take 10 percent off the top of your income to give it back to God. Some people interpret this as 10 percent of net, others as 10 percent of gross. Regardless of what you decide, God has promised to bless the tithe.

In Malachi 3:10 after telling the Israelites to bring the tithe into the storehouse, God went on to say, "Test me in this . . . and see if I will not throw open the floodgates of heaven and pour out so much blessing that you will not have room enough for it" (NIV). Go ahead and put God to the test. He will be faithful and will bless your obedience in giving.

Provision (Daily Needs)

After you give the first 10 percent of your income to God, you can take care of your daily needs such as clothing, car allowances, housing, and food. Eliminating debt and saving are also daily needs. Maybe you are wondering, how much do I need for my lifestyle? Only you can answer that question, but it should be answered with prayer, in light of making an eternal impact, and how it will affect others.

Lastly, remember God has promised to "supply all your need according to His riches in glory by Christ Jesus" (Phil. 4:19), but it's important to be a good steward of what He has given you.

Without a plan, most people live a lifestyle in keeping with their salary. As their salary grows, so does their standard of living. But living for God requires planning. Remember, your provisions are simply a way to glorify Him. Therefore, you need to have a standard of living in mind—along with a budget—for each stage of life. Do you know how you will allot your money in your twenties, thirties, and forward? Do you track your spending regularly to keep it in line with your budget plan? For future budgets, you can project most everyday expenses for the lifestyle you will pursue.

You should include getting out of debt, paying off a home mortgage, funding college educations, and saving for retirement. You will also need to know when enough is enough so that once you achieve your desired standard of living you can commit excess funds to saving or more giving. At what age would you like your investments to support you? It may be at retirement or earlier so you are free to serve God in new ways. Do you have goals for your net worth? How much do you want to accumulate by age thirty, forty, fifty, and sixty?

Offerings

The Bible says, "Let each of you look out not only for his own interests, but also for the interests of others" (Phil. 2:4). After you have taken care of your daily needs, you may have money left over to be a blessing to someone else, which is the second way God wants us to give—through offerings. An offering, like a tithe, is given to build God's kingdom by supporting a local church, a ministry, or individuals in need, such as widows, orphans, and the poor. Unlike a tithe, offerings are not required by God but are given freely and reflect the desire to glorify God and make Him known. Some offerings may be spontaneous as God reveals a specific need to you;

others should be planned as you commit to a strategy to consistently be a blessing.

My wife, Michele, has a huge heart for offerings. She loves to see the tangible results of blessing others. She would find zero satisfaction in writing a large check to support a ministry. That is something that would give me great joy, but Michele would rather be doing something to meet people's needs in measurable ways. I was proud of her when she recently rallied a group of people to collect two garages full of used clothes to support impoverished people in the Appalachian Mountains.

If we hoard God's gifts, we will miss out on the joy that comes through giving; but when we act as a channel to distribute God's gifts, we will experience His love. Financially, this begins with the tithe and then includes other opportunities to sow into His kingdom through offerings.

Offerings are your opportunity to express a heart of gratitude to God and a commitment to see His kingdom reign. Freewill gifts demonstrate something different than those that are required. How you seize these opportunities says a lot about you. God gives us talents, positions of authority, relationships, and finances to do with as we choose. When we voluntarily use them to glorify God, it proclaims Him a priority. The first commandment calls us to have no other gods before Him. Offerings allow us to live out the first commandment in a very tangible way. They show that we are not using our money to serve ourselves or someone else. They are presented directly to God as a sacrifice.

We were designed for generosity. Giving may seem like an obligation to many, but to believers it's a great opportunity. Jesus said that it's more blessed to give than to receive (Acts 20:35), and Paul wrote that God loves a cheerful giver (2 Cor. 9:7).

It only makes sense that if God is a sacrificial, generous giver, and if He's putting His nature within us as we grow to be like Him, then we will be sacrificial, generous givers too. Those who learn to give away much of what God has given them experience the fullness of His joy in ways that many other people don't. This is a spiritual secret that many people have never understood, a profound key to the ways of God's kingdom. Liberal giving is inextricably connected with spiritual maturity and joy.

To illustrate the importance of offerings, imagine that three of the thickest, juiciest steaks in the world are served up in front of you right now. These are really big ones as you'd expect from the finest steak houses. All three are identical. And all three are the tastiest cuisine available anywhere. As you sink your teeth into the first one, the value it brings is high. Not only is it satisfying your basic need for sustenance, but it's also pleasing your palate at the same time.

As you bite into the second one, the experience is somehow a little different. The pleasure is still high. But your hunger is no longer ravenous. It's not that the steak is any less able to satisfy; it's just that the need for satisfaction has already been met by the first one. So the second one is unable to deliver quite the same level of satisfaction as the first. The value is different because your need was different. Having your need for sustenance met already, the second steak represented a luxury—an indulgence above and beyond your basic needs.

Now start into the third steak, and the value it brings is even lower. At this point, your stomach is starting to bulge. Instead of enjoying the experience, you now must work to down the serving. As you chew each bite, your jaw muscles begin to ache. The texture seems different, and the meat no longer melts in your mouth. With each swallow, you begin to feel your gag reflex kicking in. Again, this steak is identical to the other two, but because your situation is now different—your primary needs are already met—the value you receive from it has been greatly reduced. In fact, it has the potential to make you sick and throw up the whole meal!

Contrary to the messages of our culture, the more abundant something becomes, the less value it has for the possessor. So here is my big question: What if you could trade your "third steak" in the form of money or possessions for the blessing of giving to others who are in great need or peril? What if, instead of adding nothing to your fulfillment, your abundance could add to the fulfillment of someone else?

If you bless others now with your excess, you'll trade it for joy. The Bible says, "It is more blessed to give than to receive" (Acts 20:35). But, the Scripture also tells us that even a cup of cold water given to someone in need will be rewarded in heaven (Mark 9:41). How can you use your "third steak," or your excess time, talent, and treasure to bless others?

Always remember, money is only as good as what you trade it for. And if you invest it in God's kingdom, you will trade it for eternal rewards.

It Doesn't Take a Lot

Perhaps you believe you have to have a lot of money to be a blessing. This is simply not true. As pastor Andy Stanley said in his teaching *Two Bags Full*, "It's not important what you have, but what you do with what you have"[3]—and everyone has something to give.

In his book *The Christian Atheist*, pastor Craig Groeschel tells a story about a time when he didn't have a lot of money but something amazing happened when God prompted him to give a small offering to a woman at church. When he was a new follower of Christ and in college, he attended church with some friends. During worship, he noticed a woman seated nearby who looked as though she had experienced a difficult life. Her clothes were worn, and premature lines etched her face. Compassion began to fill Craig's heart that started to grow. He knew God was nudging him to give her all the money he had on him, but because he had often struggled with worrying about having enough money, selfishness crept in and he hesitated. He wrote,

When I pried open my wallet, all I had was a five-dollar bill. My logical mind jumped in, That's not enough to make a difference in her life. It's only five dollars. Besides, that's the money I was going to spend on my lunch. And, I'm hungry.

As much as I tried to argue, the feeling simply wouldn't subside. *Give her all the money you have—even if it's only five dollars.* Not wanting to disappoint what I thought was God's quiet voice, I softly approached this woman, afraid I might appear to be a freak or stalker.

"Ma'am," I said gently, "I know this is going to sound strange, but I think God wants me to give this to you. I know it's not much, but it's all I have."

She glanced down at my meager five dollars, and I couldn't help feel embarrassed. Did I insult her? Would she feel humiliated? Her countenance dramatically changed. Her eyes beamed. She looked like she'd just won the lottery. She threw her hands up, smiled at the ceiling, and shouted, "Thank you, God! I love you so much!" Then she hugged me, tears streaming down her face.

I tried to just give her the bill and slip away, but she grabbed me. She explained that when she woke up earlier in the day, she desperately wanted to go to church to worship God, but as a single mom, she was out of money and wouldn't get paid until Tuesday. She had only enough gas in her car to get to church, but not enough to get home. Torn between going to church and staying home, she asked God what she should do. After a few minutes of seeking God, she felt God led her to go to church and trust him. So she put her eight-year-old son in the car and drove to church, unsure how they would get home.

When I gave her the small token of money, she knew five dollars would provide enough gas for her to get home and then some. God had miraculously provided for her. I walked away in awe of God's goodness. Then I thought to myself, *But what am I going to do for lunch?* When church was over, a friend invited me to lunch and said he was buying. Instead of my normal fifty-nine-cent tacos, my friend got me an eight-dollar hamburger. God is so good![4]

PUTTING ON THE RIGHT ATTITUDE

All that is needed to be a blessing to others is to have a giving attitude. This doesn't mean you practice *occasional* generosity. It means you ask God to give you a generous heart so you consistently notice needs around you. You'll be surprised that people everywhere need help. You may be able to buy someone a cup of coffee, give someone some of your clothes, or purchase a new car for someone. You won't be able to meet every need, but when you *do* share you will experience joy as Craig did.

Also keep in mind that giving doesn't have to be monetary. You can also give of your time, talents, and possessions. I dare you to try giving on a regular basis and see how it changes you.

MOTIVES MATTER

One Sunday Billy and Ruth Graham went to church. As the

offering plate passed by, Billy reached into his pocket and meant to pull out a five-dollar bill. He pulled out a fifty-dollar bill instead and didn't realize it until he had already placed it in the offering plate. He was surprised by what he had done. He turned to his wife, Ruth, and said, "Well, at least I will get a reward in heaven for giving fifty dollars."

"No," Ruth said, "you are going to get a reward for five dollars because that is all you meant to give."[5]

When it comes to giving, motives matter. When we give generously with a pure heart, we will be blessed. Luke 6:38 says, "Give, and it will be given to you: good measure, pressed down, shaken together, and running over will be put into your bosom. For with the same measure that you use, it will be measured back to you." This may not mean that you receive more money, but God will reward you, either now or in eternity.

Abundance

After you give a tenth of your income to God, take care of your provision, and give offerings, you may have money left over to buy something special, or invest more into God's work. This is called abundance. The word *abundance* may sound as though it only applies to rich people. However most people in the United States live in abundance. I recently read a Facebook post that said, "If you have food in your fridge, clothes on your back, a roof over your head and a place to sleep you are richer than 75% of the world. If you have money in the bank, your wallet, and some spare change you are among the top 8% of the world's wealthy."[6]

Some of us who are "wealthy" according to the above statement can pay for small extravagances like our Starbucks coffee every day. Others can afford something like a vacation home or a new car.

One thing is certain: if you follow God's priorities for money, your heart will be changed to allocate your abundance in ways that glorify Him.

How will you use excess funds you receive? Will you simply put it back into your standard of living, or do you have another plan for how you can glorify God with your resources? How much will you allot for personal ministry dreams? How much money will you allot for relationship-building experiences with your spouse, your family, your unchurched friends? Are there any personal accomplishments you hope to realize that might require a financial investment? Are there any personal pleasures you will grant yourself as part of your strategy? Your plan for abundance should also include your goals for kingdom building. Perhaps you would determine a percentage of abundance that will go to the church and a percentage you will spend on yourself. I encourage you to pray and ask God to help you define how you should spend the abundance He provides.

In closing, let me emphasize that following a solid financial plan isn't just good because Scripture says we should be wise stewards. And, it's not good just because what you do with your money can make a major impact on heaven. It's also important because it will affect your ability to carry out your calling. Do you remember the wheel we talked about in chapter 7 that emphasized that each of the Big Five need to be in balance?

Remember that when a person's finances get out of balance, everything else in their life can suffer: their relationships, their career, their spiritual life—even their calling. Remember that the more debt you have, the harder you will have to work to pay for what you own.

We can literally wear ourselves out and negatively affect all other areas of our lives when our finances get out of balance.

DISCOVERING THE FINANCIAL LIFE
YOU WERE BORN TO LIVE

As you set your goals for your financial strategy, remember you are a steward of God's resources, not an owner of your resources. Fix your gaze firmly on eternity, ordering your priorities around what will last. Always remember that the money you manage can either be spent on temporary pleasures or be leveraged for eternal gain. God wants you to be blessed financially and enjoy His gifts, but His greater goal for your finances is for you to make investments in His kingdom work, where the benefits last forever.

ETERNAL PERSPECTIVE SCRIPTURE

"And I say to you, make friends for yourselves by unrighteous mammon [worldly wealth], that when you fail [die], they may receive you into an everlasting home" (Luke 16:9).

Chapter Twelve

YOUR CAREER STRATEGY

P EOPLE'S FEELINGS ABOUT WORK RUN the gamut. Some love what they do; others loathe work and daydream about winning the lottery so they never have to work again.

If you do a Google search for the phrase "I hate my job" you'll find a plethora of Internet posts rang_ng from videos, articles, and quizzes to help those who are dissatisfied with their work.

But not everything you hear about work is negative. Popular songs often make tribute to hardwork.ng folks, and news headlines celebrate those who add value to society through their careers. Some people recognize the great value in their work and love their jobs or careers. Still others vacillate be_ween enthusiasm and dread. One week is fulfilling; the next feels like a nightmare.

What's your attitude about your job or career? Are you miserable or content? Do you have to drag yourself out of bed each morning, or do you wake up with enthusiasm? Do you count the days until the weekend, or do you feel blessed to have your job or career?

Finally, what do you believe God thinks about your work? Do you feel it is a punishment or curse? Are you convinced that God cares about your work, or do you feel that having a satisfying career is just for other people because God is more concerned about your spiritual development?

If your . . .

- main career goal is to reach a point where you can retire and lead a life of leisure,

- work is just something you suffer through until you get to
  the end of your life,
- work is anything less than a channel through which you
  bring glory to God . . . then read on.

In this chapter, I'd like to take a look at some common misconceptions about work, then help you develop a strategy for your career to support your Blueprint for Life (including the Big Five) and your calling. Let's start with two common misconceptions about work:

Work is a curse. Bob hates his career. When you ask him how he feels about it, he will say, "Well, I am just working every day so I can retire and go to heaven." What a tragic perspective! Bob is missing the point of work: that it can be a way to glorify God and make an impact on eternity. Unfortunately, a lot of men live just like Bob. They think work is a curse and just something to tolerate until Christ calls them home.

But the Bible has something different to say about work. In fact, God designed it from the very beginning. When God created Adam, Scripture says, "The Lord God took the man and put him in the Garden of Eden to work it and take care of it" (Gen. 2:15 NIV). Adam was *placed* in the garden. He didn't accidentally show up there, nor was he placed in the garden to simply enjoy it, eat fruit, and walk and talk with God. Instead, he was placed there to "work it and take care of it." Work is God's plan. It's His will. It's His gift.

Granted, we have no idea what work would have been like without the consequences of sin. Sin has certainly made everything harder—including work. But regardless, work has been a gift from God since the beginning. It's one way we can glorify God; it's our responsibility, and it was meant to be pleasing to God and a blessing to others.

Only Christian vocations matter to God, and "secular" work does not. When Becky was a new Christian, she thought if she wanted to be pleasing to God and make an impact on the world that she had to go into ministry. Many people have the inaccurate view just like Becky that ministry work matters, but secular work is meaningless. They feel their career is useless because they aren't "in the ministry." They aren't standing behind a pulpit, writing books about Christ, or rescuing orphans. As a result, they feel as if they are trapped in a daily grind of pushing papers, attending meetings, or creating spreadsheets.

Perhaps you resonate with these sentiments. I hope I can encourage you to rise above these feelings of futility by looking at your work from the following perspective:

1) The work you do is God working through you. Martin Luther once said, "What else is all our work to God—whether in the fields, in the garden, in the city, in the house, in war, or in government—but just such a . . . [way] by which He wants to give His gifts in the fields, at home, and everywhere else? These are the masks of God, behind which He wants to remain concealed and do all things."[1]

In response to Luther's statement, Timothy Keller wrote in his book *Every Good Endeavor*:

> The most modest jobs—like plowing a field or digging a ditch—
> [are] the "masks" through which God cares for us. . . . *These are
> all God's callings,* all ways of doing God's work in the world, all
> ways through which God distributes his gifts to us. Through our
> work we bring order out of chaos, create new entities, exploit
> the patterns of creation, and interweave the human community.
> So whether splicing a gene or doing brain surgery or collecting
> the rubbish or painting a picture, our work further develops,

maintains, or repairs the fabric of the world. In this way, we connect our work to God's work.[2]

Wow! Talk about a powerful perspective. Your work, my work, your neighbor's work matters to God because it is God at work through us. Keller says God could have given us the bread already baked, or the house already built. But He didn't. Instead, He has given us wheat for bread and wood to build the house. And when we work to bless God and others, God is at work through us. Keller says, "Every good work is a great work."[3]

Not only do so some people think that secular work doesn't matter, they think there are only some kinds of work that matter. Maybe you have felt this same way. Maybe a doctor or an attorney or someone with a high profile seems like they matter more than a teacher. But every good work is a great work.

In his book *66 Love Letters*, Dr. Larry Crabb provides an encouraging reminder for everyone who has wondered if their work matters: "Nehemiah did little more than build an unimpressive wall around an apparently insignificant city [Jerusalem] that has a relatively small population of unimportant-looking people. And yet, when people laughed at him for taking on such a trivial project, he replied, 'I am doing a great work' (Nehemiah 6:3 NKJV)."[4]

As if God is speaking, Crabb goes on to write:

Whatever anyone does out of a sincere desire to know me and draw others to me is a great work. And as you engage in work, sometimes you will be energized as you catch a glimpse of my plan unfolding. More often you don't. Either way you are doing a great work.

Every father who repairs a leaky faucet and then prays with his kids before dinner is doing a great work. Every mother who prepares that dinner and joins in prayer is doing a great work. Every single person who works hard to pay the rent and reads the Bible before bedtime is doing a great work. I see it all. And I am pleased. *Their reward is coming.*[5]

Indeed, He sees it all. He knows when we sit and when we rise. He knows every word before we speak it, every thought from afar, and He is familiar with all our ways (Ps. 139:1–6). The great news is that when we truly believe that God knows all and sees all and that it all matters to Him, we will be motivated to do our work with excellence to make a big impact on eternity. We can also experience the joyful reality that every good work is a great work when it's done for Christ—and our reward is coming. Therefore, we should not make light of the daily tasks He gives us and call them insignificant.

KEEPING YOUR CAREER IN ALIGNMENT

Now that we have looked at some inaccurate views of work and some answers for those views, let's dive into how you can keep your career in alignment with the other four of the Big Five and with your calling so you don't crash and burn.

Here are three things your career needs to do:

- Serve the other higher priorities in your life
- Support the other Big Five areas of your life
- Align with—never frustrate—your calling

Your career needs to serve the other
higher priorities in your life.

In a message titled "Choosing to Cheat," Andy Stanley tells a story about a hardworking man who gives his wife a rock. It's not a gift; he just needs her to hold it for a while because he has been so busy working some long hours. This rock represents their marriage and his responsibilities around the house, with the kids, and to her as a good husband. He hands her the rock and she says, "Sure, I'll help you, honey," because she loves him and wants to be supportive.

Over the next few months, the man continues to work long hours and his wife continues to hold the rock, but the rock gets heavier and heavier until one day the man comes home and his wife has dropped the rock. It has broken into a million pieces. And their relationship has broken into a million pieces too.[6]

This story is all too common. When someone's career becomes too important and doesn't remain in balance with the rest of the Big Five, their calling will suffer, their relationships will suffer, and their relationship with God will suffer.

It can be so easy for this to happen when we get kudos from work, or when the work we are doing is important. It can be especially easy to justify working too much and believe that devoting extra hours to do God's work at the expense of time with family is okay.

Granted, there may not be immediate repercussions if we ask those around us to "hold our rock." But eventually something will break, and it might be the ones we love the most. Remember, God will never put you in a position of consistently stealing time from your most meaningful relationships to accomplish career goals. There may be brief seasons when you need someone close to you to "hold your rock." Maybe you have a pressing deadline, or an unusually demanding schedule for a season; but if it's a situation you find yourself in consistently, it's a problem.

If this describes you, do what you can now to make a change. If you think you might be addicted to work, the problem is deeper than just having a demanding schedule. You may need to seek professional help. Don't forget to ask Christ to show you why you feel the need to overwork. Is it people pleasing? The desire to feel significant? To prove your value? Or is it because of problems at home? When you balance your career so that it supports the higher priorities in your life, you'll be much happier.

Your career needs to support the other
Big Five areas in your life.

Instead of asking, "Does my career choice fulfill my maximum earning potential?" we should ask, "Does my career choice allow me to leverage my skills and talents to pursue God's purpose for my life?" He doesn't always lead us to the highest-paying job. He leads us to the opportunities for greatest fruitfulness. When deciding between two employment options, the one with the best retirement plan, vacation allowance, and other benefits may not be the one that lines up with our purpose. If we focus on provision alone, we may miss our mission. But if we focus on fulfilling our mission, the provision for that mission will follow.

Like money, your career is a tool that should be used to help you serve God with your whole life. Just as your family and your church community are platforms for service, your career should also be viewed as a platform for carrying out God's work. Sometimes it's primarily a financial vehicle to fund the other areas of your life. Sometimes it's the primary vehicle through which you exercise your God-given mission in life. Most often, it's a combination of both.

Your work should never be your reason for living. Serving God is. Similarly, serving yourself should never be your reason for working. Serving God should. If your driving ambition for going to work each day is to get ahead financially or to experience the thrill of unraveling the latest challenge or to just make it to the weekend—anything other than glorifying your Creator—then you could be missing the whole point God had in mind when He created work.

Your career needs to align with—
never frustrate—your calling.

In chapter 3, I explained how your career and calling may—or may not be—the same. As with a pastor, perhaps your career and calling are identical. Or maybe your story is more like mine. Perhaps your career *supports* your God-given calling, which it always should.

Maybe you feel called into ministry or to be a portrait painter. You may need to work full-time to support your calling. That said, every career—and really every area of the Big Five—can be seen as an opportunity to fulfill God's purposes. If your job is staying at home caring for children or other family members—you, too, have vital work that God has planned for you. So your career doesn't necessarily have to be a formal career that brings in a paycheck.

God has a plan for your life's work—and that includes a plan for your career to dovetail perfectly with your calling. When it does, your career will support and serve your overall Blueprint for Life to ultimately serve His purposes.

PROVISION TO PASSION

Many people think the sole purpose of work is to provide income. Other people think the sole purpose of work is to support one's passions. There are many ideas out there about how to balance provision and passion. Some people say, "Do what you love, the money will follow." Others suggest you build a nest egg for early retirement, and then pursue your passions.

As I mentioned earlier in the book, your career should support your calling—or what you are passionate about. Or, sometimes your calling and career may be the same. Regardless, balancing passion and provision is possible on both counts. Then, it's possible to experience joy and fulfillment knowing you are living your life to glorify God.

A balanced career strategy is the best strategy. This involves asking some practical questions. Do you need your career to provide a salary? Then you should plan for that. Can you find paying work that exercises your unique skills and talents? Then you should pursue it. Is your spending under control, enabling you maximum freedom as you consider your career options? Are there non-career activities that might serve as an alternative outlet for your personal passions, freeing you up to make objective decisions about your employment?

Regardless of how we balance provision and passion, God wants us to remember that He will be faithful to meet our needs. He is our provider, blessing our work and causing it to bear fruit. And He wants us to live out of the passions He gave us to fulfill our callings.

Congratulations! You have just learned how to develop a strategy for each of the Big Five. As we finish our journey together, I want to take a look at the end of your life from a very special porch swing. I hope it will help you become even more convinced of the importance of fulfilling the special calling that God has for your life so you can glorify Him.

ETERNAL PERSPECTIVE SCRIPTURE

"For the Son of Man will come in the glory of His Father with His angels, and then He will reward each according to his works"
(Matt. 16:27).

Chapter Thirteen

A VIEW FROM THE PORCH SWING

IMAGINE YOU ARE AT THE end of your life. It's your ninetieth birthday, and you're relaxing on your porch swing. As you watch the sun set, you take a stroll down memory lane and evaluate your life. You think about the opportunities you had to glorify Christ and demonstrate your love for Him and others through your calling and the Big Five. And, you converse with the Lord about these many moments. You know you will stand before Him very soon, praise Him for His sacrifice on the cross—and you will give an account for how you have lived.

As you prepare for your end-of-life "porch swing moment," you have two options: you can look back knowing you loved and glorified Him with your whole heart or you can look back in regret. Author Anne Lamott wrote in her book *Bird by Bird: Some Instruction on Writing and Life*:

> What if you wake up some day and you're 65, or 75, and you never got your memoir or novel written; or you didn't go swimming in warm pools and oceans all those years because your thighs were jiggly and you had a nice, big comfortable tummy; or you were just so strung out on perfectionism and people-pleasing that you forgot to have a big, juicy creative life, of imagination and radical silliness and staring off into space like when you were a kid? It's going to break your heart. Don't let this happen.[1]

In this quote, Lamott is talking about squeezing the life out of every moment and every opportunity, about saying yes more than you say no, about keeping a young spirit that is ready for adventure, even as our hair grays, our body ages, and our days accumulate. She is talking about *living*.

What does a juicy life, a life that is not filled with regret at the end, look like for the Christ follower? It's got to be about more than just having fun, keeping a youthful spirit, writing one's memoir, or going to beach parties.

For the Christian, living a juicy life that doesn't result in regret while sitting on one's "porch swing" means making an intentional plan to live for Christ. It means looking beyond our present, earthly reality to our sobering reality that one day we will stand before Christ and we will answer for how we stewarded our lives. It means deciding not to be ordinary, but to be extraordinary for Christ. It means giving yourself away.

We know Christ will review our lives and will "render to each one according to his deeds" (Rom. 2:6). Thankfully, we don't have to wait to see Him face-to-face after death to evaluate if we have lived for Him.

Imagine tomorrow is the day you will stand before Jesus. You know that loving Christ and demonstrating that love for Him through pursuing your calling and thereby blessing others is important to Him.

Would you say so far that it's been worth it? Have you loved Him with your whole heart and glorified Him the best you can with your life? Thankfully, it's never too late to start living for Christ. As long as you still have breath, God has work for you to do; He has a calling for your life. To glorify God through your calling and to avoid looking back in regret, here are some closing thoughts to keep in mind.

Count the Cost

I recently read that some dog breeds are so intelligent they can understand more than twelve hundred words. When I heard about a golden retriever named Pumpkin, I wondered if she understood more than just words, but could also comprehend how invisible fences work.

Life is pretty good for Pumpkin. She can roam freely around her owner's two-acre country yard. She can smell the roses, dig holes, and chase her sister-dog—all inside an invisible fence. But if she wanders outside the fence, she receives a little shock as a reminder not to go outside her boundaries.

The first few times Pumpkin received a zap, it kept her inside the yard. But then one day Pumpkin's owner, Sam, saw her chasing the neighbor's rabbits—outside the invisible fence. Once Sam dragged Pumpkin back home, he kept a close eye on her to figure out how she had managed such an incredible feat.

Pumpkin, the smart pooch, figured out if she ran fast enough at the invisible fence, she could bust through and it wouldn't hurt. For Pumpkin, it was all about risk and reward. The risk of getting zapped was not as threatening as the potential reward of catching a rabbit was exhilarating.

Some people say, "Well, I don't believe in eternal rewards. I don't believe that it matters what I did on earth." They think all that is required is to accept Christ into their hearts, believe that He died on the cross for their sins, and that's it. My question for them is this: What if I am right about eternal rewards? If I am, they have lost everything. But if I am wrong, then they haven't lost a thing! I challenge you to seriously consider the claims I have made in this book on eternal rewards. I challenge you to pray and ask God if loving Him and glorifying Him through the Big Five is a big deal to Him. When you believe that everything you do matters to God and this belief impacts how you live your life on a day-to-day basis, you will be well on your way to experiencing excitement for what's coming in eternity.

ACCEPT RESPONSIBILITY

Sometimes people think, *Well, it's my choice how I live my life, if I fulfill my calling and use my gifts and passions. It's my choice if I let fear hold me back, the criticism of others stop me, or my desires for the things of this world prevent me from doing God's will.* True. It is your choice, but you have a responsibility. In fact, we all have a responsibility to steward well what God has given to us to glorify Him and serve others.

Can you imagine a bird who says, "No, I will not sing" or a fish who says, "I will not swim"? God made you purposefully with the gifts and talents you have so you could *use them,* not waste them.

In Matthew 25:14–15, Jesus said, "For the kingdom of heaven is like a man traveling to a far country, who called his own servants and delivered his goods to them. And to one he gave five talents, to another two, and to another one, to each according to his own ability; and immediately he went on a journey."

As the story unfolds, one man is given five talents. He doubles it by being a good steward over it and investing it. The man with two talents does the same. But the man who had received just one talent doesn't do anything with the talent he has been given. He buries it in the ground instead.

In his book *Driven by Eternity*, John Bevere wrote, "A talent is a measure of money, but since this is a parable it likely means the parable represents something else. One possibility, which I personally believe true, is the level of our call and gifts."[2]

When the Master returns the first two men—the one with five talents and the one with two talents—are rewarded. And the master—who in this story is Jesus—says, 'Well done, good and faithful servant; you were faithful over a few things, I will make you ruler over many things. Enter into the joy of your lord" (v. 21).

But to the one who buried his talent in the ground, the master says, "You wicked and lazy servant, you knew that I reap where I have not sown, and gather where I have not scattered seed" (v. 26). Then the master takes the talent he does have and gives it to someone else.

We have all been given gifts to use just like the servants in the story. My gifting doesn't look like your gifting. But when you look back on your life, God won't measure your impact by if you fulfilled your wife's calling, or your neighbor's calling, or your pastor's calling. God will reward you according to your calling and how you stewarded the gifts He gave you.

Bevere added, "There are certain individuals who have levels of ministry to reach nations, others that reach cities, and still others who reach home groups within the church. Another example could be some writers who reach millions, others who reach thousands, and still others who reach hundreds. Still another could be a person possessing an administrative gift that could bring a ministry to a megachurch level, while others could only handle churches of intermediate or smaller sizes."[3]

IT'S FOR OTHERS

In chapter 4, I mentioned 1 Peter 4:10, which says, "As each one has received a gift, minister it to one another, as good stewards of the manifold grace of God."

This scripture reveals the beautiful truth that our calling is not just about making us happy or finding a purpose for living so we are comfortable. Instead, every person God has created has received a gift, for the benefit of the body.

This scripture also reveals that when we use the gift we have received, we are being good stewards of God's grace. In other words, people receive God's grace through the gifts we exercise.

According to Thayer's Lexicon, the word *grace* in this verse is the word *charis* in the original Greek language. *Charis* is defined as "the merciful kindness of God, exerting his holy influence upon souls, turns them to Christ, keeps, strengthens, increases them in Christian faith, knowledge, affection, and kindles them to the exercise of Christian virtues."[4]

Therefore, it's when we use our gifts that others receive God's grace. Through our gifts, we are stewards of His grace whereby God influences people, strengthens them, changes them, and showers His affection on them.

Do you see that if you don't do what God has called you to do and use your gifts that you are robbing not only God but also others? There are people in this world who need you. You have been created to make a difference for Christ through your calling that will positively impact the world.

Ask the Right Questions

The good news is that you don't have to look back at your life with regret. Since you know that one day you will look back on your days either from your "porch swing" or with Christ, why not plan to live intentionally now?

Here are some questions you can ask to evaluate how you might feel while looking back from your "porch swing."

- Will you smile as you remember how you pursued life with courage and an adventurous spirit for Christ?
- Will you be confident that you loved your spouse sacrificially the way God intended?
- Will you know you poured yourself into your children and that you cultivated precious memories with them, and seized every moment you could with them to demonstrate your love?
- Will you be confident that you made the most of your career? Will you know you leveraged it as a way to support your God-given calling?
- Will you be satisfied with your generosity toward others? Will you know you did all you could to share your excess blessings with those in need—or will you live with the regret of spending all of your resources on yourself?
- Will you be satisfied with the way you prioritized your life by placing God first, relationships second, and career third?

- Will you have had an intentional strategy to cultivate meaningful and healthy relationships?
- Will your accomplishments live long after you breathe your last breath?
- When you stand before Christ will you be confident that He will say, "Well done, my wise and faithful servant"?
- Most importantly, will you know you lived faithfully in close relationship with the God who made you?

BEGIN WITH GOD

The last and most important thing to remember so you can look back in confidence is to remember that anyone who wants to live for Christ begins with Christ. Just as a helicopter can't fly without a propeller, a fish can't swim without water, and a bird can't fly without wings, you can't fulfill your true calling apart from Christ.

John 8:32 is an oft-quoted scripture. In it, Jesus said, "You shall know the truth, and the truth shall make you free." Many people throw this phrase around as if truth is just good information, and if you know information that you will experience freedom. But a clear look at John 8:31–32 shows that experiencing freedom is a direct result of following Christ: "To the Jews who had believed him, Jesus said, 'If you hold to my teaching, you are really my disciples. *Then* you will know the truth, and the truth will set you free'" (NIV, emphasis mine).

Freedom is always preceded by holding to Christ's teaching or being a disciple.

216

Here's how it works:

- First you must become Jesus' disciple.
- Then you hold to His teaching.
- As a result you will know truth and be set free to be all God has called you to be.

Being a disciple means that you are more than just a learner or pupil. A disciple is someone who accepts instruction given to him by God to make it his rule of conduct. In fact, the word *disciple* is derived from a word that means "to learn by putting what one learns into practice." Therefore, intellectual knowledge is not the measure of discipleship. Action is the measure of discipleship.

What does this have to do with not living a wasted life and not looking back in regret? In the same way that you can't experience freedom unless you know the truth that comes from being in relationship with Jesus, you can't live out your calling and comprehend the truth you need to manage the Big Five apart from relationship with Jesus.

If you want to be free to pursue God's calling for your life so you don't look back in regret, first you must give Him your life and become His disciple. You cannot live out your true calling apart from Christ. So in the same way that you can't discover truth that leads to freedom without being connected to Christ or discipleship, you can't discover your purpose without being in relationship with Christ.

If you don't know Christ, I invite you to invite Him into your life at this time. Here is a prayer you can pray to begin your relationship with Him.

Dear God,

I come to You in the name of Jesus. I acknowledge to You that I am a sinner, and I am sorry for my sins and the life that I have lived; I need Your forgiveness.

I believe that Your only begotten Son, Jesus Christ, shed His precious blood on the cross at Calvary and died for my sins, and I am now willing to turn from my sin.

You said in Your Holy Word, Romans 10:9, that if we confess the Lord our God and believe in our hearts that God raised Jesus from the dead, we shall be saved.

Right now I confess Jesus as the Lord of my soul. With my heart, I believe that God raised Jesus from the dead. This very moment I accept Jesus Christ as my own personal Savior and according to His Word, right now I am saved.

Thank You, Jesus, for Your unlimited grace that has saved me from my sins. I thank You, Jesus, that Your grace never leads to license, but rather it always leads to repentance. Therefore, Lord Jesus, transform my life so that I may bring glory and honor to You alone and not to myself.

Thank You, Jesus, for dying for me and giving me eternal life.

Amen.

If you prayed this prayer to invite Christ into your life, I invite you to send us a note from our website, Blueprintforlife.com.

The next step is to find a church home to fellowship with other believers and study His Word. It will be the best decision you have ever made.

Will you build your Blueprint for Life to make your life count? Will you be confident as you face your "porch swing days," or will you look back with deep regret?

Remember: God will reward you for what you have done for Him as stated in Revelation 22:12: "And behold, I am coming quickly, and My reward is with Me, to give to every one according to his work."

I challenge you. Don't live an ordinary, status-quo life. Make an impact for God now and you'll make an impact for eternity.

ETERNAL PERSPECTIVE SCRIPTURE

"I press toward the goal for the prize of the upward call of God in Christ Jesus" (Phil. 3:14).

ACKNOWLEDGMENTS

THIS BOOK IS DEDICATED FIRST to my Mom and Dad, who gave me a loving Christian home where many of these ideas and principles were learned and nurtured. Second, to my good friends Boyd Bailey and Hal White, who spent many hours working with me to refine these biblical life principles that are embodied in this book. Finally, to both Ben Ortlip and Shana Schutte for providing their God-inspired talent to help write these words so beautifully and clearly for all to read.

NOTES

Chapter One

1. Bruce Wilkinson, *A Life God Rewards* (New York: Doubleday Religious Publishing Group, 2012), 44–45.

Chapter Two

1. "Chapter 1: Amazing Facts About the Universe," BreadofLifeBibleStudy.com, accessed November 10, 2014, http://www.breadoflifebiblestudy.com/Lessons/28God'sCreation/Articles/Creation03.pdf.
2. Rick Warren, *The Purpose Driven Life* (Grand Rapids, MI: Zondervan, 2002), 17.

Chapter Three

1. "Dr. Tony Evans, The Importance of Calling," YouTube video, posted by True Word of Yeshua, February 3, 2014, http://www.youtube.com/watch?v=seJNSXmGyvQ.
2. Ibid.
3. Sparky Anderson, "Goodbye," special insert in the *Detroit News*, published September 27, 1999.
4. David DiSalvo, "8 Reasons Why People Feel Lost in Their Lives," *Forbes*, posted September 9, 2012, http://www.forbes.com/sites/daviddisalvo/2012/09/19/8-reasons-why-people-feel-lost-in-their-lives.

5. Ken Robinson, *The Element* (New York: Penguin Group, 2009), 33–34, 48.
6. Interview with Tom Turco. Royal Family Kids' Camp Director. Boise, Idaho, 2005.

Chapter Four

1. John Maxwell, "Leaders Develop Daily, Not in a Day," JohnMaxwell .com, accessed November 10, 2014, http://www.johnmaxwell.com /cms/images/uploads/ads/Leaders_Develop_Daily_Not_in_a_Day .pdf.
2. "Tim Keller - Why Work Matters," YouTube video, posted by RedeemerCFW, May 18, 2012, http://www.youtube.com/watch?v =rTVIvdBIuLE.

Chapter Five

1. Jack Canfield, *A Third Serving of Chicken Soup for the Soul: 101 More Stories to Open the Heart and Rekindle the Spirit*, 3rd ed. (Deerfield Beach, FL: Health Communications, 1996).
2. Randy Alcorn. Video. *The Doctrine of Eternal Rewards* http://www .epm.org/resources/2013/Mar/27/doctrine-eternal-rewards/
3. Joni Eareckson Tada, *Heaven: Your Real Home* (Grand Rapids: Zondervan, 1997), 110.
4. *Gone with the Wind*, directed by Victor Fleming, Sam Wood, and George Cukor (1939; Burbank, CA: Warner Home Video, 2000), DVD.
5. John Bevere, *Driven by Eternity* (Brentwood, TN: Faithwords, April 10, 2006), 205.
6. Ibid.
7. Pastor Tony Evans, Facebook post, February 22, 2014, https://www .facebook.com/pastortonyevans/posts/753357548010681.

Chapter Six

1. Kathy Lamancusa, *Condensed Chicken Soup for the Soul* (Deerfield Beach, FL: Health Communications, 1996), 152.
2. Mark Batterson, *Draw the Circle: The 40 Day Prayer Challenge* (Grand Rapids, MI: Zondervan, 2012), 47.
3. Ibid.

Chapter Seven
1. Timothy Keller, *Counterfeit Gods* (New York: Penguin, 2009), ix.
2. Ibid.
3. *"How to Live a Balanced and Blessed Life*: Part 1," by Charles Lowery, Vimeo, posted by Cross Church, July 12, 2010, http://vimeo.com/13270460.

Chapter Eight
1. "Bill Hybels – Coffee with God," YoutTube video, posted by StudentImpact, August 4, 2010, . http://www.youtube.com/watch?v=-xU9GR4H0WQ.
2. Anne Graham Lotz, "Journey to Jesus: Learning to Hear His Voice," AnneGrahamLotz.org, accessed November 11, 2014, http://www.annegrahamlotz.org/resources/topic/all-bible-studies/learning-hear-his-voice.
3. Wendy Blight, *Living So That* (Nashville, TN: Thomas Nelson, 2014), 35.
4. Mark Batterson, *Draw the Circle* (Grand Rapids, MI: Zondervan, 2012), 67.
5. Warren G. Bennis and Robert J. Thomas, *Geeks and Geeezers: How Eras, Values, and Defining Moments Shape Leaders* (Watertown, MA: Harvard Business School Press 2002), 19.
6. Elmer Towns, *God Encounters* (Delight, AR: Gospel Light Publishing Company, 2000), 15.
7. John MacArthur, "The Lonely Ember," accessed January 15, 2015, http://www.inspirationalarchive.com/texts/topics/evangelization/lonelyember.shtml.
8. Lanny Donoho, *God's Blogs* (Colorado Springs, CO: Multnomah Books, 2005), chapter 6.
9. Dan Millman, Patty Hansen, *Condensed Chicken Soup for the Soul* (Deerfield Beach, FL: Health Communications, 1996), 4.

Chapter Nine
1. iDisciple.com, "Loving God Means Loving Others," by John Eldredge, published by Ransomed Heart Ministries, accessed November 11, 2014, https://www.idisciple.org/post/loving-god-means-loving-others.
2. Timothy Keller, *The Meaning of Marriage* (New York: Penguin Group, 2011), 50.

3. Ted Lowe, "The Best Thing for Your Kids is For You to Leave." Blueprintforlife.com, posted March 5, 2014, http://blueprintforlife .com/blog/the-best-thing-for-your-kids-is-for-you-to-leave.

4. Carol Ummel Lindquist quoted by Teri Cettina in "How to Save Your Marriage from Your Kids," CNN.com, posted July 29, 2009, http:// www.cnn.com/2009/LIVING/personal/07/29/p.stronger.marriage .secret/index.html.

5. Dr. Philip C. McGraw, *Relationship Rescue* (New York: Hyperion, 2001), 292.

6. Bob Goff, *Love Does* (Nashville, TN: Thomas Nelson, 2012), 128.

7. Ibid.

Chapter Ten

1. John MacArthur, *Anxious for Nothing* (Colorado Springs, CO: David C. Cook, 2012).

2. "How Much Does God Want Me to Care for My Physical Body?" by John Piper, YouTube video, posted by Indy Long, August 1, 2012, http://www.youtube.com/watch?v=YCoUTeVjZSA.

3. Lysa TerKeurst, *Made to Crave* (Grand Rapids, MI: Zondervan, 2010), 89.

4. Ben Opipari. "Need a Brain Boost? Exercise," *The Washington Post*, posted May 27, 2014, http://www.washingtonpost.com/lifestyle /wellness/need-a-brain-boost-exercise/2014/05/27/551773f4-db92 -11e3-8009-71de85b9c527_story.html.

5. "A Christian Looks at Depression – Tom Nelson" YouTube video, posted by dallasseminary, May 8, 2012, http://www.youtube.com/watch?v =jXecSlwVBTQ; Jill Ewert. "Christians and Depression" *Sharing the Victory*, January/February 2009, http://archives.fca.org/vsItemDisplay .lsp&objectID=1D097539-158C-4998-9A47400933E65011.

6. National Sleep Foundation, "Sleepy Connected Americans," SleepFoundation.org, posted March 11, 2011, http://sleepfoundation .org/media-center/press-release/annual-sleep-america-poll-exploring -connections-communications-technology-use-.

Chapter Eleven

1. Sandy M. Fernandez, "6 Beliefs About Money That Can Cost You." DailyWorth, posted on Yahoo! Finance, July 15, 2013, http://finance .yahoo.com/news/6-beliefs-money-cost-000000856.html.

2. Randy Alcorn, *The Treasure Principle* (Colorado Springs, CO: Multnomah Books, 2009), 9.
3. Andy Stanley. Video Message. "Two Bags Full" (February 26, 2012) http://northpoint.org/messages/comparison-trap/two-bags-full.
4. Craig Groeschel, *The Christian Atheist* (Grand Rapids, MI: Zondervan, 2010), 177–178.
5. "Our Motive in Giving," *Greg Laurie Daily*, Harvest.org, posted March 15, 2006, http://www.harvest.org/devotional/archive/devotion /2006-03-15.html.
6. Facebook.com, posted by Beauty, Brains, and Beyond, December 15, 2011, https://www.facebook.com/BeautyBrainsAndBeyond/posts /218458518230545.

Chapter Twelve

1. Martin Luther, "Exposition of Psalm 147," in *Luther's Works*, vol. 14.
2. "Tim Keller – Why Work Matters" Youtube video, posted by RedeemerCFW, May 18, 2012, http://www.youtube.com/watch?v =rTVIvdBIuLE.
3. Ibid.
4. Larry Crabb, *66 Love Letters* (Nashville, TN: Thomas Nelson, 2009), 73, (emphasis added).
5. Ibid, 74, emphasis added.
6. Andy Stanley, "Choosing to Cheat," Northpoint.org, accessed February 4, 2015. http://northpoint.org/messages/breathing-room/ choosing-to-cheat.

Chapter Thirteen

1. Anne Lamott, *Bird by Bird: Some Instruction on Writing and Life* (New York: Anchor Books, 1994).
2. John Bevere, *Driven by Eternity* (Nashville, TN: Faithwords, 2006), 229.
3. Ibid.
4. *Thayer's Greek Lexicon*, "5485. Charis," BibleHub.com, accessed November 10, 2014, http://biblehub.com/greek/5485.htm.

ABOUT THE AUTHOR

MICHAEL KENDRICK IS A SENIOR partner and cofounder of Roswell Capital Partners, his Atlanta-based investment banking firm. Kendrick has twenty years of experience in the investment banking and fund management fields. In 1999 Kendrick founded Ministry Ventures Inc., a nonprofit organization dedicated to launching new ministries for Christ. Since that time, Ministry Ventures has been instrumental in launching more than forty new Christian, nonprofit organizations. Kendrick also serves as CEO and President of the Blueprint for Life ministry organization. Blueprint for Life publishes books, small group materials, and an online daily devotional designed to encourage others to live a life of purpose in light of eternity.

Kendrick is a founding member and former elder of North Point Community Church, a 30,000-member church led by Andy Stanley. Kendrick has and continues to serve on a number of nonprofit boards in Atlanta, and his family regularly provides mission and service work to a variety of causes. In addition to his two recently authored books, *The Fulfillment Factor* and *Rich Forever*, Kendrick developed an innovative eight-week discipleship study course called

"Blueprint for Life," which focuses on living life intentionally with an eternal perspective.

He holds a master's degree in business administration from Embry Riddle University and a bachelor's degree in aerospace engineering from Auburn University. Michael and his wife, Michele, live in Alpharetta, Georgia, with their three children.